The **Essential** Buyer's Guide

ALFA ROMEO GIULIA
SPIDER

Your marque experts: Keith Booker
& Jim Talbott

T0386711

VELOCE PUBLISHING
THE PUBLISHER OF FINE AUTOMOTIVE BOOKS

Also from Veloce Publishing

www.veloce.co.uk

First published in October 2005 by Veloce Publishing Limited, Veloce House, Parkway Farm Business Park, Middle Farm Way,
Poundbury, Dorchester, Dorset, DT1 3AR, England. Reprinted January 2014 & March 2021
Tel 01305 260068/fax 01305 250479/e-mail info@veloce.co.uk/web www.veloce.co.uk or www.velocebooks.com.

ISBN: 978-1-904788-98-0 UPC: 6-36847-00398-2

British Library Cataloguing in Publication Data – A catalogue record for this book is available from the British Library.
Typesetting, design and page make-up all by Veloce Publishing Ltd on Apple Mac. Printed and bound by CPI Group (UK) Ltd,
Croydon, CR0 4YY.

Introduction

The purpose of this book is to offer a quick step-by-step guide to assessing a Giulia Spider, with the aid of a unique marking system. The information and guidance should enable you to have confidence in your purchase and to negotiate a fair price. The photographs are intended to represent what you might find when examining a car that is for sale.

Superb 1600 Kamm tail Spider Junior. (Courtesy Stuart Braley)

Established in 1910, Alfa Romeo is one of the world's oldest motor manufacturers, with an unrivalled sporting heritage. Prewar, the cars were very much hand built, often based on the company's highly successful competition cars. Postwar, Alfa Romeo gradually established itself as a volume manufacturer, starting with its first monocoque, the 1900. This was joined in 1954 by the smaller 1300cc Giulietta, manufactured in saloon/sedan (Berlina), coupé (Sprint), and open two-seater (Spider). The 1600 105 series Giulia saloon/sedan, was launched in 1962, with the Sprint and Spider continuing, but fitted with the larger engine. The Sprint was replaced in 1964; the Spider in 1966.

The traditional layout of the 1750 Spider Veloce long tail.

The 105 Giulia Spider was the last design of Battista 'Pinin' Farina, evolving from the 'Super Flow' exercises of the late 1950s.The latter were based on the competition 6C3500 cars and had very sleek fronts and rears with distinctive side scallops. The Giulietta Spider Speciale Aerodinamica designs, revealed in 1961, were very close in style to the Duetto, but it took another five years for the production car to be launched. Initially the motoring press was not complimentary about its shape, considering it contrived when compared to the model's very attractive predecessors. The press and the public soon warmed to it, however, and it became a favourite, particularly in the United States. Although prototype Spiders based on the Alfetta were shown in the mid 1970s, they never made it to production, and the Giulia 105 Spider continued until 1993, some 16 years after it was due for replacement! Its

Where it all started ... the 1600 Duetto.

chic, timeless design and advanced technical specification make it one of the most sought-after classic sports cars.

Thanks
The authors would like to thank:
Alan Bennett of Benalfa Cars
Roger Dykes of Willows Restorations
David Edgington and Kevin Abigail of E B Spares
Roger Evans of Peak Alfa
Bruno Giacomelli
Richard Norris of ClassicAlfa
Elvira Ruocco, Head of Alfa Romeo Historical Documentation Centre, Milan
Mike Spenceley of MGS Coachworks
Stuart Taylor of the AROC Giulia 105 Register
Among those whose cars appear in this book are:
Stuart Braley
Enzo Cucchiara
Mark Ferri
Louise Northern
Peter Vaughan

Essential Buyer's Guide™ currency
At the time of publication a BG unit of currency "●" equals approximately £1.00/US$1.40/Euro 1.16. Please adjust to suit current exchange rates.

Contents

1 Is it the right car for you?
– marriage guidance

Tall and short drivers
Tall drivers with long legs may need the seat as far back as possible, which will restrict the view of the nose and necessitate looking through an unswept area of the windscreen. They may find that their heads protrude above the top of the windscreen when the hood is down. Seats have good fore/aft and backrest adjustment. Steering column is non-adjustable.

Weight of controls
Heavier than modern cars, particularly steering at low speeds on non-power assisted cars.

Will it fit in the garage?
Length 168in, width 65in (4.25 x 1.63 metres). Allow 8-9ft garage width (2.5-2.7 metres). Driver's door is largish, and has to be opened a reasonable amount to enable driver to get out of the car with hood up.

Interior space
Very comfortable for two. Rear 'seat' area suitable for storage only.

Luggage capacity
Room in boot/trunk for two large soft bags, plus space around for oddments. This is lockable via the 'B' pillar.

Running costs
Fuel consumption is 20-32mpg, 8.5-10.6kpl, depending on engine size. Mechanicals and service items are reasonably priced; body maintenance/care is expensive.

Useability
Larger engined cars cope well with modern conditions. 1300s are 'buzzy' at motorway speeds. Front and rear panel and side scallops vulnerable to parking damage. With hood up, rear quarter vision restricted.

Parts availability
Nearly all mechanicals available. Body parts are expensive with some limited availability.

Insurance
All Spiders are over 10 years old, so classic car limited mileage insurance is available. Owners' Clubs are often able to offer competitive everyday cover.

Investment potential
There's always a demand for good quality Spiders. Prices rise as parts availability improves.

Foibles
Rear end can break away in the wet when car is pushed on tight corners. Floor mounted pedals on early cars take some getting used to.

Plus points
A famous manufacturer; stylish, timeless appearance. Sophisticated mechanical specification for age. Good performance, handling and feel of controls. Excellent design enables maximum use of soft top.

Minus points
Scuttle shake on some cars, harsh ride at slow speeds, electrics can be unreliable, weak 2nd gear synchro.

Alternatives
Triumph TR4/5/6, Lotus Elan, MGB, Jensen Healey, Fiat 124 Spider.

Soft top down and enjoying the sun with fellow Alfa enthusiasts!

Note: Labour costs will vary greatly
Small service cost: 3750 miles (6000km) ● x100-150 approx.
Large service cost: 11,250 miles (18,000km) ● x300-400
approx.
New clutch, fitted, parts & labour: ● x250-300.
Rebuilt engine, parts & labour: ● x1800-2500.
Rebuilt gearbox, parts & labour: ● x500.
Unleaded head conversion: most specialists state that these
cars can run on unleaded without modification/adjustment.
Only consider if rebuilding head anyway. US cars are designed
to run on unleaded.
Brake disc: Dunlop F & R: ● x100, pads (complete set):
● x60. ATE F & R: ● x28-35, pads: ● x35 (per set).
New headlight: each ● x18; bowls ● x45.
Headlight cowls: ● x40.00. Rear lights each: ● x90-120
depending on model.

Rear lights are
available but can
be expensive.

Complete body restoration: ● x8000-15,000.
Full respray (including preparation): ● x3000-5000, depending
on panel condition.
To fit wing: front or rear: ● x600-1000.
Body seals: ● x180-200 (excluding soft top).
Hood/soft top: ● x 250-350.
Parts that are easy to find: All
mechanical, shock absorbers, brakes,
electrics, service parts, glass, seals,
exhausts.
Parts that are difficult to find: All
long-tail Spider panels (repair panels
required to fit later items) and brightwork,
S3/S4 bumpers. Some body panels for
S2.
Parts that are expensive: Bumpers,
front & rear wings, rubber mat sets.
nose repair panels, doors, rear lights.
The parts supply situation changes
constantly.

Panels like these may not always be
available.

3 Living with a Giulia Spider
– will you get along together?

Good points

With its timeless Pininfarina styling, an Alfa Romeo Spider is a visual delight. It is one of the world's most admired, two seat open sports cars, as popular today as when it was in production. Within twenty-eight years of manufacture there should be a model to suit everyone. If you're looking for a classic to pamper and use on hot, sunny days, the elegant, long-tailed Spiders from the late 1960s/early 70s may be for you; a Series 3 or 4 will meet the needs of someone who wants to use the car more often, perhaps everyday; the 1750 and 2000 Kamm tails are a good compromise between the two.

Soft top is easy to use.

With a well-proven, all-aluminium, twin cam engine, five speed gearbox, all round disc brakes, double wishbone front and well located rear suspension, combined with precise steering and excellent throttle response, a good Spider is a pleasure to drive. Like most Alfas, the harder you push a Spider, the better it rides and responds. With an easy to use soft top and an excellent heater, an owner can enjoy open air motoring throughout the year. It's a comfortable car for two people and their luggage and, whilst the driving position will not suit everyone, most soon adapt to it. A Spider's major mechanical components are robust, if properly maintained, and an excellent network of specialists provides support.

Bad points

Compared to its more 'agricultural' contemporaries, a Spider – with its advanced specification – will have required greater care and attention over the years. In many cases it will not have received this, and so suffered neglect and abuse. It is important, therefore, to exercise caution when buying one and ensure that you continue to look after it properly. A local garage may not be able to help with this, so you will need to make a little extra effort to keep it up to scratch.

Compared to modern cars, the gearbox will feel notchy and slow when starting from cold, especially if the second gear syncromesh is worn. The steering, on non-power assisted models, will feel heavy when manoeuvring and in traffic. This, combined with awkward pedal angles on some models, will make slow driving hard going. In such conditions, Spiders fitted with carburettors, will often 'oil' their plugs, requiring a burst of high revs to clear.

The brake and clutch pedal on this Duetto are bottom hinged and can seem awkward to operate at first.

Although some later Spiders are fitted with lower profile tyres which provide good grip, earlier cars with higher profile rubber demand a degree of respect when pushed hard in the wet. Until you get used to it, the slight flexing of the bodyshell, particularly with the hood down, will feel quite strange. This, combined with scuttle shake, which is worse on some models, will make you aware that the basic design is 40-plus years old.

When parking, it can be difficult to judge the length and position of the long nose, which can result in damage to the bodywork and the low slung sump. Rear vision with the hood up is not good, particularly if the plastic rear window is in poor condition. Getting in and out of a soft top car is not quite as straightforward as with a GT or saloon/sedan, but, in this respect, a Spider is no worse than its contemporaries. The latter comment also applies to wind noise. Convertibles are prone to water ingress; however, take extra care when checking this out in case it indicates a more sinister problem.

Practicalities – will it suit your lifestyle?

You will be the best judge of this, and it will depend on what you require from a Spider. Many today are bought as fun cars to be used when the weather is warm and dry. As this model gets older, fewer and fewer will be used on a day-to-day basis. Jim Talbott has covered over 100,000 miles in his 1991 Series 4 Spider, including everyday use, over many years. It has always been maintained by specialists and has had regular 'Waxoyl' top-ups. The only major mechanical repairs have been a cylinder head overhaul at 95,000 miles, and a transmission rebuild. It has needed only a small patch of welding in the 'heel area' of the floor pan. A more sporting feel has resulted from the fitting of uprated rear springs and Bilstein shock absorbers designed for this model, improving ride and reducing scuttle shake. The car is fun to drive, with enough power for modern conditions. A fast run, with the soft top down on good, non-motorway roads, is exhilarating, and a drive home from work after a stressful day will nearly always lift the spirits.

Boot space is adequate for the luggage of two people.

Room behind seats is adequate for stowage of soft bags and oddments.

The Spider enjoyed a production life of twenty-eight years, more than twice that of the Giulia GT coupé, with which it shared much of its running gear. During this time it underwent many changes; some more desirable than others. Cars exported to the USA – although looking similar to those sold in other markets – differ significantly, which can affect their value outside that country. Only the 1600 Duetto and Series 4 models have similar specifications for both markets. (See Chapter 12 for value assessment and Chapter 16 Vital statistics for more information.) Listed below, in percentage terms, are the relative values of individual models in relation to the UK market. Local markets may differ considerably.

1600 Duetto – the original long-tailed Spider.

Note: From 1975 (US and 1.6 from 1972) all models have a 115 model designation, except RHD cars which remained as 105 series until production ceased in 1977. US cars did not have headlamp cowls but broad rimmed chrome headlamp bezels instead.

Kamm tail. This is the 1600 Junior.

1600 Spider Duetto-1570cc. Made in RHD/LHD. Long, rounded tail. Exported to the USA in small numbers. 1966-67: **100%**

1750 Spider Veloce-1779cc. Made in RHD/LHD. Similar in appearance to Duetto. Exported to USA. 1967-69: **100%**

1300 Spider Junior-1290cc. RHD/LHD. Visually similar to Duetto but no headlamp cowls or bezels. Not exported to USA.1968-69: **80%**

1750 Spider Veloce Kamm tail-1779cc (subsequently known as Series 2). Made in RHD/LHD. First short tail model with increased windscreen rake. Continued in various styles, on subsequent versions. Exported to USA. 1970-71: **90%**

The elegant front of the Series 2 Kamm tail.

1300 Spider Junior Kamm tail-1290cc. LHD only. Similar in appearance to 1750 but no headlamp cowls or bezels. Not available in USA. 1970-77: **60%**

1600 Spider Junior/1600 Spider Veloce Kamm tail-1570cc. LHD only. Appearance as 1300, SV as 2000. Not exported to USA. 1972-81: **65%**

2000 Spider Veloce Kamm tail-1962cc. Made in RHD/LHD. Similar to 1750. RHD manufacture ceased in 1977. Exported to USA where cars have extended chrome bumpers and overriders, changing to prominent rubber bumpers with a

US specification Series 3 Spider Veloce.

The last fascia incarnation featured on late Series 3 and S4 Spiders.

token Alfa shield from 1975. US limited editions: Niki Lauda and Enthusiast's models.1971-82: **90%**

2000 Spider Series 3 (Aerodinamica)-1962cc. LHD only (RHD cars converted). Euro cars without headlamp cowls but broad bezels. Plastic front and rear bumpers/coloured coded front and large black rear spoiler. Exported to US. Lower spec US limited edition was called 'Graduate'. 1983-89: **65%**

1600 Spider Series 3-1570cc. LHD only (RHD cars converted). Appearance as per 2000. Not exported to USA.1983-89: **60%**

2000 QV Green Cloverleaf Series 3-1962cc. LHD only (RHD cars converted). Exported to USA. As per Series 3 but fitted with colour coded body kit.

The very full engine bay of this Bosch injected Spider Graduate.

1986-89: **70%**

2000 Spider Veloce Series 4-1962cc. LHD only (RHD cars converted). Complete re-style with integrated body coloured bumpers/grille/side skirts, kicked up boot/trunk lid and wrap around rear lights . Two-tone 'Beaute' and US 'CE' special editions. 1990-93: **80%**

1.6 Spider Series 4-1570cc. LHD only. Offered in some European countries. Similar appearance to 2000. 1990-92: **75%**

Works hard top fitted to this late Series 4.

Series 3 Green Cloverleaf (QV) basks in the sun.

5 Before you view
– be well informed

To avoid a wasted journey, and the disappointment of finding that the car does not match your expectations, it will help if you're very clear about what questions you want to ask before you pick up the telephone. Some of these points might appear basic but when you're excited about the prospect of buying your dream classic, it's amazing how some of the most obvious things slip the mind ... Also check the current values of the model you are interested in in classic car magazines which give both a price guide and auction results.

Where is the car?
Is it going to be worth travelling to the next county/state, or even across a border? A locally advertised car, although it may not sound very interesting, can add to your knowledge for very little effort, so make a visit – it might even be in better condition than expected.

Dealer or private sale?
Establish early on if the car is being sold by its owner or by a trader. A private owner should have all the history, so don't be afraid to ask detailed questions. A dealer may have more limited knowledge of a car's history, but should have some documentation. A dealer may offer a warranty/guarantee (ask for a printed copy) and finance.

Cost of collection and delivery
A dealer may well be used to quoting for delivery by car transporter. A private owner may agree to meet you halfway, but only agree to this after you have seen the car at the vendor's address to validate the documents. You could meet halfway and agree the sale but insist on meeting at the vendor's address for the handover.

View – when and where
It is always preferable to view at the vendor's home or business premises. In the case of a private sale, the car's documentation should tally with the vendor's name and address. Arrange to view only in daylight and avoid a wet day. Most cars look better in poor light or when wet.

Reason for sale
Do make this one of the first questions. Why is the car being sold and how long has it been with the current owner? How many previous owners?

Left-hand drive to right-hand drive conversions
A number of Series 3 and Series 4 cars were imported into the UK and converted to right-hand drive by Bell and Colvill. S4 Spiders were sold through the dealer network in LHD initially, but an Alfa Romeo approved conversion by Seaking was

subsequently offered. (Identified by a plate in the B pillar on the driver's side.) RHD cars, of a specification not usually seen in the UK, sometimes appear eg: Kamm tailed Junior Spiders. They have usually been imported from South Africa, Singapore or Australia. Thoroughly check out before dismissing and take care when examining other conversions.

Condition (body/chassis/interior/mechanicals)
Ask for an honest appraisal of the car's condition. Ask specifically about some of the check items described in Chapter 7.

All original specification?
An original equipment car is invariably of higher value than a customised version.

Matching data/legal ownership
Do VIN/chassis, engine numbers and license plate match the official registration document? Is the owner's name and address recorded in the official registration documents?

For those countries that require an annual test of roadworthiness, does the car have a document showing it complies (an MOT certificate in the UK, which can be verified by the DVSA on 0300 123 9000 or online at gov.uk/check-mot-status)?

If a smog/emissions certificate is mandatory, does the car have one?

If required, does the car carry a current road fund licence/licence plate tag?

Does the vendor own the car outright? Money might be owed to a finance company or bank: the car could even be stolen. Several organisations will supply the data on ownership, based on the car's licence plate number, for a fee. Such companies can often also tell you whether the car has been 'written off' by an insurance company. In the UK these organisations can supply vehicle data –

HPI: 0113 222 2010
AA: 0800 056 8040
DVLA: 0844 453 0118
RAC: 0330 159 0364
Other countries will have similar organisations.

Unleaded fuel
Injected US cars are designed for this fuel. Most specialists agree that Spiders will run on unleaded, without modification/adjustment. Upgrading often takes place with a cylinder head rebuild. If modified, ask for details and recommended fuel.

Insurance
Check with your existing insurer before setting out as your current policy may not cover you to drive the car if you do purchase it.

How can you pay?
A cheque/check will take several days to clear and the seller may prefer to sell to a cash buyer. However, a banker's draft (a cheque issued by a bank) is as good

as cash, but safer, so contact your bank and become familiar with the formalities necessary to acquire one.

Buying at auction?
If the intention is to buy at auction see Chapter 10 for further advice.

Professional vehicle check (mechanical examination)
There are often marque/model specialists who will undertake professional examination of a vehicle on your behalf. Owner's Clubs will be able to put you in touch with such specialists.

Other organisations which will carry out a general professional check in the UK are:

AA 0800 056 8040 / www.theaa.com/vehicle-inspection (motoring organisation with vehicle inspectors)

RAC 0330 159 0720 / www.rac.co.uk/buying-a-car/vehicle-inspections (motoring organisation with vehicle inspectors)

Other countries will have similar organisations.

6 Inspection equipment
– these items will really help

This book
Pen/pencil and notepad
Reading glasses (if you need them for close work)
Magnet (not powerful; a fridge magnet is ideal)
Torch
Probe (a small screwdriver works very well)
Overalls
Mirror on a stick
Digital camera
A friend, preferably a knowledgeable enthusiast

Before you rush out of the door, gather together a few items that will help as you work your way around the car. This book is designed to be your guide at every step, so take it along and use the check boxes to help you assess each area of the car you're interested in. Don't be afraid to let the seller see you using it.

Take your reading glasses if you need them to read documents and make close-up inspections.

A magnet will help you check if the car is full of filler, or has fibreglass panels. Use the magnet to sample bodywork areas all around the car, but be careful not to damage the paintwork. Expect to find a little filler here and there, but not whole panels. A torch with fresh batteries will be useful for peering into the wheelarches and under the car.

A small screwdriver can be used – with care – as a probe, particularly in the wheelarches and on the underside. With this you should be able to check an area of severe corrosion, but be careful – if it's really bad the screwdriver might go right through the metal!

Be prepared to get dirty. Take along a pair of overalls, if you have them. Fixing a mirror at an angle on the end of a stick may seem odd, but you'll probably need it to check the condition of the underside of the car. It will also help you to peer into some of the important crevices. You can also use it, together with the torch, along the underside of the sills and on the floor.

If you have the use of a digital camera, take it along so that later you can study some areas of the car more closely. Take a picture of any part of the car that causes you concern, and seek a friend's opinion.

Ideally, have a friend or knowledgeable enthusiast accompany you: a second opinion is always valuable.

7 Fifteen minute evaluation
– walk away or stay?

Before viewing a car and to avoid a wasted journey, you need to be satisfied that the information given to you by the seller is correct. If you're looking at a Spider being sold privately, it's best to view it at the seller's home so you can verify the address.

After a brief evaluation of the main problem areas, you will be able to decide whether to proceed to a more detailed examination. It is always good to remember the following advice:

Don't let the heart rule the head

Don't buy the first car you look at, unless it is truly outstanding

Don't be influenced by the seller's sales talk

Don't be afraid to walk away

Don't be pressurised into making a decision

Most Spiders will have had several owners and the degree of care they will have received may have varied. A car may also have been well used and exposed to salt. Soft tops are vulnerable to water ingress, and the Spider has many built-in rust traps. Most models had poor corrosion protection from new, and the true condition of a car may not be apparent until it is cut apart!

A bodily sound example with suspect mechanicals is preferable to one with a rebuilt engine and poor bodywork Always buy the best you can afford. It is usually cheaper to pay a fair price for a well-restored example than a middle or low price for one needing work. In many ways running a Spider today is easier than in the past as a result of improving parts availability. If you need to budget for fixing things that you've discovered, allow at least double your first estimate!

Know what you're looking at

If you know someone who owns a Spider ask them if they will go along to see the car with you. This is where becoming a member of an Owner's Club can be so helpful: contact details appear in Chapter 16 The Community later in the book. Clubs are a rich source of information, and many have a Giulia 105 series register with people pleased to offer advice or who may know the car you are looking at.

If you have studied data, road tests and photographs, you should know what to expect. Beware of 'mix and match' cars, because Giulia engines are interchangeable and essentially look the same. As engine sizes increased, the manufacturer upgraded other mechanical components to match, ie: 2000s have bigger brakes and a limited slip differential. Many 1300s have been fitted with larger engines, but have smaller brake discs and a lower top gear. Check that the engine number matches the model type. (See Chapter 17 Vital statistics.) If it doesn't, ask what other upgrades have been carried out. It's important that all documentation reflects a non-standard capacity engine; if you do decide to buy such a car, arrange the insurance precisely for the specification of the vehicle, otherwise you may find your cover is invalid. This applies equally to a car that has had non-standard modifications, whatever they may be.

Early American Spiders are fitted with a lot of clean air equipment, which can seriously impair performance, and they may also have been converted to carburettors. Check this is legal in your state. If a catalyst is required, is it still in place?

In the 1980s and '90s many of these Spiders were imported into the UK from California, and a steady trickle of cars enter the country from Italy and other EEC countries. These can be sound examples, though this may not always be the case; additionally, specifications varied from market to market. Ensure you know what you're looking at, and check the car's legality. Take care with any car converted to right-hand drive! (See recognised conversions in Chapter 5.)

If you're really lucky the original handbook may come with the car.

The legalities

At this stage ask to see the car's official registration documents (logbook, pink slip or equivalent), which will show the owner's name and address, and detail the car's licence number, chassis/VIN make, model and, perhaps, date of original registration. Ask for evidence of the seller's identity. If local registration requires the vehicle to have a certificate of roadworthiness, such as the MoT in the UK, ask to see that too.

Be certain that the person offering the car for sale is legally entitled to do so. The legalities involved in importing a vehicle can be complex. If the car was first registered abroad ask searching questions about what procedure was followed. It may not even be registered in your country and tax may be due!

Keep the registration documents to hand so that you can check the numbers under the bonnet (hood) when you're looking over the mechanical components. Make a note of them and any other pertinent details.

Exterior

Apart from late cars, it is almost certain that most Spiders will have had at least one respray. The paint code sticker would have originally been stuck to the underside of the boot (trunk) lid and may still be present. As already mentioned, corrosion protection on '60s and '70s cars was virtually non-existent, so it's very rare for an original early car to survive to this day, unless pampered, rust-proofed, and little used. Most cars, therefore, will have been part or fully restored. Establish what degree of restoration and maintenance has been done, when, and who did the work. If a bodywork restoration has been carried out by one of the recognised Alfa Romeo specialists, the car is almost certainly worth a look. It is more likely, though, that the car has received piecemeal repairs, often of a superficial nature, performed by people of varying skill and expertise. Although S3/S4 cars have better quality metal and protection, they still need care.

What is your first impression of the car; does it look scruffy or well cared for? If you're not deterred at this stage, examine the bodywork a little more closely. Rust can be present just about anywhere, so carry out magnet tests on any suspect areas.

View the bodywork from all angles and note any flaws. Look down the flanks of the car from the front and rear, checking that the side scallops align horizontally and vertically. Look for creasing and ripples, possibly indicating filler or poorly fitted patch panels. Examine the rust vulnerable rear wheelarches. Is the profile correct? If not, it may not just be filler but the result of a rear end impact. The front panel is vulnerable to parking damage, so check there is an even gap between it and the bonnet (hood). When looking at the car from the front, check the symmetry of the panel work, particularly around the headlamp scallops. Check the profile of front and rear valances, and for corrosion. Check for even gaps around the boot (trunk) lid and the lid itself. The door gaps should be even: too wide could be the result of a weak inner structure, accident damage or poor repairs (particularly when fitting new sills). Closed up gaps usually indicate filler.

Wheelarches are prone to rust so examine them carefully.

Most importantly, check the bottom 6in/15.5cm of the bodyshell. As a rule, signs of external rust usually indicate more problems underneath. Your first priority should be the sills (rockers), the most important part of a Spider's structure and the most expensive to repair. It is possible to check the bottom edge of the inner, middle and outer sills by feeling underneath each side. If there's evidence of serious corrosion, ie: holes, rough surfaces/filler, now may be the time to walk away. The outer sills (rockers) can be checked visually for signs of blistering and cracked filler. Originally there would have been a seam between the sill (rocker) and the front wing. If this joint is flush, it could possibly be the sign of a bodged repair. Check the condition of the wings (fenders) and look everywhere for signs of corrosion, particularly in front of and behind the wheelarches. Examine the doors, particularly underneath and around any fittings. Check the bottom of the 'A' post area, which you will need to later examine in detail,

Good panel fit is vital.

Check sills, jacking points, and location of rear trailing arm.

and inside and outside the fuel filler cap. Is the drain tube and rubber boot in place? Do the bumpers (fenders) look straight and undamaged? Plastic bumpers may have cracks and crazing. Check all the brightwork, badges and lights.

Is the soft top torn, ripped, faded or shrunk? Is there a good seal with the glass, windscreen and bodyshell? The 60 minute check in Chapter 9 will involve a thorough examination of the Spider's underside, but at this stage you may want to look under the car from each side, possibly using a mirror on a stick. Pay special attention to the critical area where the rear trailing arms attach to the underbody. Serious corrosion here may mean that the car is beyond saving.

If you've not been put off by now proceed to check out the interior.

Interior

Like most soft top cars, Spiders are never entirely waterproof, and a musty smell inside is a sure sign that water has entered the car. This can be due to poor seals, a hole in the floor or sills, or blocked and split front scuttle and/or soft top recess drain hoses. Ask the seller if you can check under the floor covering and soundproofing. Examine the floor where you can, particularly the foot wells. Can you see daylight? Drain holes exist in each foot well and also in the area behind the seats. These drain holes should all be fitted with a rubber grommet that can trap moisture, creating corrosion, which often allows it to fall out, producing a larger hole. It is often possible to weld a repair plate in place, though a complete floor panel – not always possible – may be required. Look under the floor covering overlaying the sill (rocker) on the driver's side and examine the condition of the inner sill (rocker). If all appears sound then switch your attention to seat condition.

Check the seats for the correct contour and collapsed foam. All seat material is prone to splitting, especially along the seams: S4s have especially poor quality trim. Replacement upholstery is available so don't be too deterred if this is the only problem you find.

Examine the dashboard and centre console, where fitted, for cracks, which may be repairable. Check that all instruments are present and appear sound. Check the soft top is dry inside as it may have lost its waterproofing. Good quality replacements are available.

Mechanical

When examining the mechanical aspect of a Spider, it's important to remember that good visual condition is not always indicative of mechanical soundness. Concours winners are judged on appearance and not the veracity of mechanical parts, so even when looking at one of these, you need to proceed with the same degree of care as with a lesser car. The impression you form when the bonnet (hood) is lifted will give you a good idea of how the owner has cared for the entire car; a grubby engine bay can be a big let down.

This injected engine is dusty but it's nothing that a good steam clean wouldn't put right.

With the bonnet up, look for the engine number. This is stamped low down on the left-hand side of the engine, next to the flywheel. A Spider's vehicle identity/model/type approval/chassis number plate, etc, vary from model-to-model, but can be located on the front bulkhead; some also have the chassis plate on the windscreen upright. Later Spiders have the body number on the front bulkhead, whilst the chassis VIN number is on a plate inside the windscreen and on the 'B' pillar. US cars have additional data located here. Carefully check all of these details against the vehicle documentation. In Chapter 17 Vital statistics you will find a summary of the factory model type and matching engine prefix. Numbers which don't match the documents would certainly be cause for enquiry, but don't be too concerned if the car has had an engine change at some point during its life, especially if it has undergone a full

Engine number (arrowed), stamped next to flywheel.

restoration. Remember, however, the advice given in 'Know what you are looking at' if engine capacity has changed. Seek answers to and confirmation of any anomalies, and be sure you know what size engine is in the car!

Pull out the dipstick and check the level and condition of the engine oil. Dirty oil and a low level indicate a lack of care. Ask what specification oil is in the car. Ideally, the engine oil and filter should be changed every 3000/4000 miles (6000km). If there is sludge on the dipstick, this could be the sign of a blown head gasket. Make sure you reseat the dipstick when replacing, or oil will squirt out when the engine is started. Before removing the radiator or expansion tank cap, ensure that the engine is cold. Check for 'mayonnaise' around the inside of the cap and the neck of the radiator or tank, which could also indicate a head gasket problem. Look at the water level and for evidence of anti-freeze in the coolant (colour). Check how many brake servos are fitted: early Duettos and 1300 Junior Spiders had no servo, unless aftermarket fitted. Be wary of a car that has had a larger engine but does not have a servo as braking may be compromised. Remember; larger engined cars were also fitted with bigger brake discs.

Examine brake disc condition through the holes in the wheels. If the car has been standing for a while these could have a discoloured surface, or worse still, be corroded beyond use.

Ask the seller if you can start the engine so that it can warm up. Don't ask for a test drive at this stage but listen for smoothness when idling, noisy ancillaries, and look for fluid leaks.

Look under the engine and rear axle for dripped oil.

Taking care not to dent the bodywork, press down on each corner of the car to check for suspension creaks, and that the shock absorbers control the rebound to a single smooth movement. Lighter springs are fitted at the rear, which can soften with age. This leads to sagging and gives the car the appearance of being down at the back. New springs will be needed to correct this.

Chassis number is stamped on front bulkhead on this model.

US cars have the chassis number and info in door jam and on a plate on the windscreen.

Model plate on bulkhead. Identify by referring to Chapter 17 Vital statistics.

Is it worth staying for a longer look?

Does the car appear very sound and apparently require little work? If it's a restoration case you're considering, are you prepared for all the work and expense involved? Are you able, both in terms of time and money, to take on a 'rolling restoration'? Do you have the necessary skill and expertise, or know some knowledgeable person who could assist you at a reasonable cost? A brief look at as many as possible of the foregoing points and a clear head should be sufficient for you to decide whether you are going to walk away or stay.

8 Key points
– where to look for problems

Buying a car in excellent condition, like this 1600 Junior, will save you money in the long run.

This car will present more of a challenge and will need loads of TLC!

This rust bubbling will be just the tip of the iceberg and will require major work to rectify.

This rear arch has gone beyond the repair panel stage; a complete new wing will be required.

This is what the front valance should look like – shown here during restoration.

A nicely restored rear valance. Also visible here is the fuel tank and spare wheel well.

Seats tend to split along the seams but replacement covers are available.

It's possible to check the bottom edges of the three sill panels by feeling underneath each side.

This is what the roll bar mounts and front spring pans should look like.

Frontal damage or corrosion may be evident in this area.

Look for a sound trailing arm mounting on the rear suspension.

9 Serious evaluation
– 60 minutes for years of enjoyment

Circle the Excellent, Good, Average or Poor box of each section as you go along. The totting up procedure is detailed at the end of the chapter. Be realistic in your marking!

Use a magnet to check metalwork for filler.

Good quality repair panels can be welded in.

Exterior

Bodywork condition is the most important thing to bear in mind when buying a Spider, as virtually all mechanical parts are available and straightforward to deal with. New or good quality pattern body panel supply is in a constant state of flux with many panels unobtainable: check with specialists (many of whom offer worldwide mail order) for the most up-to-date information after making an assessment of what is required (which will give you a good idea of what the repairs may involve). Good quality weld-in panels have been produced which allow a competent bodyshop to make excellent repairs or modify available panels to fit. This is often a time-consuming process and therefore can be expensive. Long tailed Spiders are very difficult and require a lot of work.

Paintwork   4 3 2 1

Series 3 and 4 Spiders are probably the only models that may still have original paintwork. Most other models will have undergone a partial or total respray, often of dubious quality; Alfa reds, dark blues, and some metallics are particularly vulnerable. Overspray on the window surrounds and brightwork indicates a low cost repaint. Refer to Chapter 14 Paint problems.

Lifting the floor covering here will expose the inner sill and floor area.

Body panels (sills/rockers)   4 3 2 1

The structural integrity of a Spider will depend upon the condition of the three-piece sills. During the 15 minute check you will have initially assessed the three sill panels by feeling underneath the car, visually checking the outer sill and with a magnet. Outer sills are sometimes replaced on their own, concealing serious corrosion. A seam would have originally existed between the outer sill and the front wing. If this is missing it could be the result of bodging, although some restorers make a flush join when fitting new sills, so check carefully.

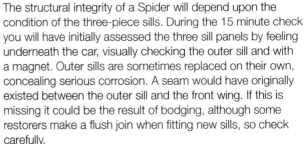

Lift the floor covering and examine the inner sills along their entire length. Probe any suspect areas with a screwdriver. Check around the seat belt anchor points as corrosion can cause them to 'pull through' in an accident. Feel under the sills, once more to re-check for rough surfaces, holes, etc. The middle sill panel will usually be fine if the others are in good condition. Sill replacement is an expensive and comprehensive exercise, requiring removal of lower adjoining wings. Bracing is required between the 'A' and 'B' posts to prevent the car 'folding' in the middle. S3QV/S4 models fitted with plastic covers are difficult to assess until the ramp check is carried out.

Body panels ('A' post base area) 4 3 2 1

Closely examine the areas around the 'A' post (the vertical pressing on which the doors are hinged). The crevices behind the splash guards (often missing) harbour moisture and dirt, resulting in corrosion of the inner and outer wings, sills, and bulkhead. These are expensive and difficult areas to repair. Minor bubbling of the wing (fender) is usually just the tip of the iceberg. Plastic arch liners on Series 4s should keep the area completely dry.

With the splashguard behind the front wheel removed, it's possible to see the mud traps.

Body panels (doors) 4 3 2 1

Do the doors open and shut and latch easily? Try opening and closing them a couple of times. Check that they fit flush with the bodywork. Examine the undersides for rust: are the drain slots clear? If it's necessary to clear them, you can be sure that moisture has lain inside the door bottoms and internal corrosion is likely. Check all the seals. Are they in good condition, or perished and compressed? Old, tired seals let in rainwater and add to noise.

Check that the drain slots in the door bases are clear.

Body panels (bonnet/hood area) 4 3 2 1

Lift the bonnet (hood). Check that the inner wings (fenders), are the same colour as the outers, and look for signs of corrosion or accident damage, particularly around the inner front panel. Filler found around the front of the car is likely to indicate old accident damage. Look down beside the engine at the front suspension mountings, the inner wings, and chassis parts that should be visible. Do they appear sound? Carefully tap the inner wings with the handle of a screwdriver. Look for corrosion in the seams of the inner wings at each end of the engine bay. Bosch injected cars have a very full under-bonnet area, so a mirror on a stick will help. Fluid leaks

Carefully check the inner wings – easier on earlier cars which have less under the bonnet/hood.

may have removed paint, exposing areas around reservoirs to corrosion. Check the front bulkhead area. The actual bonnets (hoods) are not particularly vulnerable to rust, but the leading edge is often damaged in front end accidents, or by careless parking. Check for dents and creases.

Body panels (front scuttle area) [4] [3] [2] [1]

The scuttle area is drained by two hoses which exit through the bulkhead and/or inner front wings. These can become blocked or be in poor condition, causing a build-up of water which promotes corrosion in the front bulkhead and inner wings. Water ingress to the interior through the air vents causes damage to the rear of the dashboard and keeps the carpets wet! If the owner agrees, pour some water through the ventilation grille and check it exits only from under the car.

If the owner agrees, pour some water through the ventilation grille and see where it goes!

Body panels (wings/fenders) [4] [3] [2] [1]

Examine the wings in detail using your magnet: check for irregular surfaces (a sign of filler) and corrosion. Look for rust blisters around the headlights and side repeaters. Check the lower areas, especially in front of and to the rear of the wheelarches. Missing or damaged splashguards in the front wings will permit the build-up of mud. Double skinning, build-up of moisture, and blocked drain holes will create problems. Split or blocked drain hoses from the soft top recess to the sills will affect the rear wings, particularly behind the 'B' pillars where drain hoses run from the recess to the sill. These are often in poor condition. In the event of a rear end accident, the rear wheelarches are designed to act as crumple zones so merit close attention. Sweating between the inner and outer skins make them extremely vulnerable to rust. It is helpful to compare the profile with contemporary photos. Run a hand around each wheelarch and check carefully for corrosion or filler. Exceptionally original cars may still have the factory spot-welds along the lip of the wheelarch, but it is more likely that a repair panel has been let into the metal.

Check the condition of the lower front wing and valance.

A wheelarch repair panel can be let into the rear wing.

This splashguard should keep mud away from the 'A' post base area.

Body panels (boot/trunk lid area)

☐4 ☐3 ☐2 ☐1

Protruding luggage can distort the shape
of the boot (trunk) lid. Lift the rubber seals on the boot
aperture and look underneath for corrosion. Check the boot
lid's trailing edge, which is particularly vulnerable on long
tailed Spiders. Does the lid fit flush with the surrounding
panels? Compressed seals will allow water ingress. Check the
operation of the lid and the boot lid rods. Repair panels are
available.

Body panels (valances)

☐4 ☐3 ☐2 ☐1

The front and rear valances, below the bumpers, are prone
to rot. A sound front valance is important, as it protects the
location point for the anti-roll bar. Some replacements and
repair panels are available. Rear panels on long tail Spiders are
vulnerable and notorious for holding water. The comprehensive
plastic bumpers on Series 3 and 4 Spiders envelope these
areas, providing better protection. A closer examination can be
made during the ramp check.

The front valance
is important as
it protects the
location points for
the anti-roll bar.

Body panels (shut lines)

☐4 ☐3 ☐2 ☐1

View the car from each side again, and consider the shut lines
and side scallop alignment. Door gaps should be consistent,
as should those around the boot (trunk) lid and bonnet. The
large heavy doors can drop on their hinges, causing a poor fit.
Other, more serious causes of uneven shut lines are accident
damage, weak or improperly fitted sills.

Replacement script
is available.

Body panels (exterior trim)

☐4 ☐3 ☐2 ☐1

Virtually all brightwork is available from specialists but can be
costly. Bumpers are expensive. Long tailed Spider bumpers
are hand made. Scripts crack and go black with age. Look
for rust bubbles around badge fixings. Check that the correct
items for the car are in place. Examine all plastic/rubber
trim on later cars for cracking, sagging, fading, and poor
paintwork. Electric mirror shells are particularly vulnerable as
the aluminium mounting posts corrode and lose their paint.

Round mirrors suit
early cars but can
tarnish, and rust
can appear around
mounting.

Soft tops

☐4 ☐3 ☐2 ☐1

Soft tops attach to the top of the screen by two over-centre
catches and fold into a recess behind the rear seats, where
they are held in place by either Velcro or rubber straps. A
tonneau/soft top cover keeps everything neat. Hoods are
made from proofed cotton or vinyl on some late models.
Check for rips, tears, fading, and shrinking. Rear windows are

Electric mirror
shells are
particularly
vulnerable.

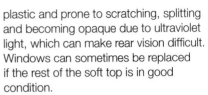

plastic and prone to scratching, splitting and becoming opaque due to ultraviolet light, which can make rear vision difficult. Windows can sometimes be replaced if the rest of the soft top is in good condition.

Slightly lower the side windows, releasing the windscreen catches, and fold back the hood/soft top. Does it move freely? Is the frame seized? Welds may break (a difficult repair with the fabric in place). Check the seals,

A tonneau or hood cover helps keep things neat.

particularly on the leading edge hood rail. This should fit in a channel, which may be badly rusted. Does it feel crunchy and uneven? Replacement is best left to a competent trimmer. The side glass should fit under the edge of the hood, which provides some guttering. Poor seals will add to wind noise. Good replacement hoods are not expensive. The condition of the hood recess drain hoses is important and difficult to assess without dismantling the rear trim. If the owner agrees pour some water around the rear of the hood and check it exits through the sills. (Not possible with long tailed Spiders.)

Wipers

Check the condition of the headlamp cowls where fitted, and also the headlamps themselves.

The wipers on long tailed Spiders have an unusual 'clap hands' movement. Subsequent models have a conventional pattern; left- or right-hand sweep (until 1977). Cars converted to right-hand drive retain a left-hand pattern, which can leave an unswept area on the driver's side. Is the wiper motor noisy, and do all speeds and intermittent facility – where fitted – work?

Glass

Are there chips, cracks or scratches in any of the windows? Being a low car, windscreens are more vulnerable to damage, especially in the driver's eye-line, a reason for MoT failure in the UK. Some Series 3 Spiders have a radio aerial built into the screen. Check the condition of the windscreen rubber and surrounding trim. Replacement screens and glass are currently readily available.

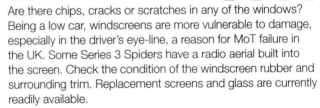

Side marker lights on rear of S2 Enthusiast's Special Edition US Spider.

Lights

Check all lights for function and lenses for chips and cracks. Headlamps are vulnerable, but cheap to replace. Cowls, where fitted, should be in good condition, so that they do not diffuse light. Headlamp bowls rot away if wheelarch splashguards are missing or damaged. Side repeaters (four different shapes) rot, but are easy to replace. US cars have wing or bumper mounted marker lights. Always check an imported car meets domestic regulations. Series 3 and 4 rear light clusters are expensive. A malfunctioning light might simply be due to a failed bulb, rusty earth/ground point, or loose connection in the fusebox. Bulbs are easy to replace and can be upgraded with a more modern specification unit.

Are the tyres the correct size and rating for the model? Note the knave plates. (Courtesy Stuart Braley)

Tyre condition and rating 4 3 2 1

Are the tyres the correct size and rating for the model? Chapter 17 Vital statistics lists original fitments. If a different specification tyre has been fitted, is it suitable for the wheel? Are all the tyres the same specification and brand, especially those on the same axle? Look at the depth and coverage of the remaining tread, and for cracks and bulges in the sidewalls. Are there any signs of age-related deterioration? If the front tyres are worn unevenly, suspect worn suspension or steering parts. Steering alignment may require adjustment.

A set of well-chosen alloys can enhance appearance.

Wheel condition 4 3 2 1

Are the wheels the standard steel items or Alfa Romeo alloys? The latter were optional extras from Kamm tailed Spiders. Some late cars and many US Spiders have them fitted as standard. Are all the wheels of the same type? Look for signs of kerbing and any other damage. Early cars have hubcaps of varying designs; later ones have 'knave plates' with exposed wheel nuts. Replacements are available from specialists. Check that aftermarket alloys are suitable for your car. Tyres or wheels which differ from standard must be declared to your insurer.

The hub plates fitted to the Duetto.

Wheel hubs & steering joints 4 3 2 1

Grip each wheel in turn and test for any free play in the hub bearings or steering joints. Ask if it's possible to have the car jacked up to do this. Investigate in more detail anything that concerns you if you proceed to the ramp check.

Interior
Floors 4 3 2 1

Check the soundness of the entire floor pan, where accessible. Tap the floor with the handle of a screwdriver to check its soundness. Is the rubber grommet present each side? Sliding the seats forward and lifting the floor covering may enable you to examine the rear foot wells, also fitted with grommets. If this is difficult, make a note to examine the area during the ramp check.

Gearlever (gearshift) gaiter (boot)   4️⃣ 3️⃣ 2️⃣ 1️⃣

Both parts of the gearlever gaiter – the outer leather/PVC item, and the rubber inner part – are prone to splitting, allowing gearbox and road noise, and engine fumes into the cabin. Replacements for both are available. Various styles of gear knob were fitted during the Spider's production.

Seats   4️⃣ 3️⃣ 2️⃣ 1️⃣

Spiders were fitted with several styles of PVC or leather seats. Early cars had vertical

Seats can wear, too!

pleating; later ones horizontal. Green Cloverleafs/ Series 4s had their own style. Token 'rear seats' changed to a shelf from 1979. Check that the seats are correct for the car as this can affect value. Headrests were fitted in most markets from 1968. Seats are prone to splitting along the stitching, and the foam diaphragm of the base can compress. Excellent retrims are available from specialists, but can be expensive. Fragile seat back hinges and frames crack easily. Check seats slide on their runners: if rusty, this can point to problems underneath.

The rubber floor covering is expensive to replace.

Carpets   4️⃣ 3️⃣ 2️⃣ 1️⃣

Embossed rubber matting was fitted until 1977 and then various types of carpet. Green Cloverleafs have red, Series 4s beige or black carpet, prone to rapid deterioration, particularly in the oversill area. Good quality replacements are available. New rubber sets are expensive.

Carefully check the door cards.

Door cards   4️⃣ 3️⃣ 2️⃣ 1️⃣

Various styles have been fitted. Warped cards are usually a result of missing or torn door gaskets, resulting in the backing rotting and water ingress. Are the armrests secure and/or split? Replacements are available, but check availability and cost.

Door locks   4️⃣ 3️⃣ 2️⃣ 1️⃣

Check function, both inside and out. Replacements are obtainable from specialists.

Door handles   4️⃣ 3️⃣ 2️⃣ 1️⃣

Long tailed Spiders and Kamm tailed Juniors have push button handles. Flush fitting, teardrop-shaped items were

The push button door handles fitted to long tail Spiders and Kamm tail Juniors.

fitted to subsequent models. These are hinged at the rear, and if not adjusted correctly can be difficult to operate. Later cars have rubber gaskets which give a better seal with the door skin. Handles are made of poor quality metal and tend to blister, scratch easily, and lose their finish: replacements are available. Check the operation of the door release lever.

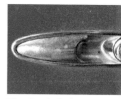

The flush-fitting handles can lose their finish.

Window winders

Do they function smoothly, and are handles secure? Do electric windows raise and lower at a reasonable speed, without noise or scratching? It's not unusual for electric motors to become slower prior to giving up the ghost completely. Always fit new regulators when renewing. Little used quarterlights can seize, with the glass sticking to the rubber. Carefully check they are operational. Juniors have fixed quarterlights.

Steering wheel

Early models have plastic rimmed, aluminium spoke wheels, fitted with horn push buttons; Duettos three spokes, Juniors two. From the 1750 to early Series 3 Spiders, a thin, wood rimmed wheel, also with push buttons, appeared. This was dished to help alleviate the 'long arms' problem. Initially, the spokes had an aluminium finish which changed to satin black. From 1986 a new wheel – with three, thick black spokes and a large plastic centre boss – was fitted, with stitched PVC or leather rims. US Series 4 Veloces have a 4-spoke wheel with an airbag.

Series 3 fitted with a smart aftermarket steering wheel. Note the single instrument pod.

Instrument panel

Long tailed Spiders and Kamm tailed Juniors have body coloured, steel painted facias with the main instruments contained within a plastic binnacle in front of the driver, and minor ones centrally mounted at an angle. Series 2s and early Series 3s have a plastic moulded facia with two recessed cowls for the main instruments, and, again, centrally mounted, angled minor ones. From 1986 all instruments and warning lights were contained within a single pod in front of the driver. Look for damage underneath and around all areas of the facia: cracks and splits can sometimes be repaired. Check that all instruments are present and function, with working

US spec S2 with standard wheel and cowled main instruments.

backlights. Condensation should soon clear when on the move. Check that the heater slides are working.

Handbrake (parking brake) [4] [3] [2] [1]

If the car has not been used for a while, the handbrake can seize. Check the ratchet action by easing the lever up and down. If the lever appears to come up too far, the cable could be stretched, or adjustment may be needed. Dunlop-braked cars are difficult to adjust for good efficiency. Check gaiter condition.

Pedals [4] [3] [2] [1]

Early left-hand drive and all factory right-hand drive Spiders have floor mounted

brake and clutch pedals. These take some getting used to, as does the 'long arms, short legs' driving position. The pedals are quite close together, and those with broad feet should be careful not to depress two simultaneously! Hanging pedals were fitted to all LHD Spiders from the Kamm tail revisions. Is the wear on the pedal rubbers consistent with the mileage reading? Have they been replaced? Are they secure? Look, too, at the condition of the rubber gaiter surrounding the pedal box.

Hanging, top hinged pedals.

Boot (trunk) interior [4] [3] [2] [1]

Depending upon the model, boot floors will either be carpeted or have fitted rubber

The battery was located in the boot on Bosch injected versions.

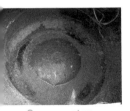

Severe water damage in this spare wheel well.

'Alfa Romeo' embossed mats. Does the boot smell musty and damp? With a long boot lid – flat in most models – condensation can build up underneath and the resultant water drips onto the floor covering, creating damp. Compressed seals and rot around the aperture will also allow further water ingress; ideal conditions for rot!

Lift the floor covering. Is the boot floor dry? Check the inner wings and the seams between the floor, inner wings and rear panel. Check for kinks in the boot floor, a sure sign of accident damage. Check for corrosion around the battery on fuel-injected cars. Lift out the spare wheel and check for corrosion in and around the well. Is the rubber grommet, which enables water to be drained, still in place? Are there any other holes? The entire well can rot through but replacements are available.

Check the fuel tank, the channel around it, and the filler neck.

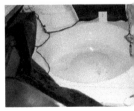

No problems if the spare wheel well looks like this!

Check around the channel where the petrol tank is secured – another rust trap! In really bad cases, rust will have caught hold throughout the boot area; a difficult repair although new panels can be found. Is there a smell of petrol? A replacement tank – only recently available – may be required. Look to see if the rubber seal, where the fuel filler neck meets the petrol flap, is in good condition. If not, this may result in petrol fumes. Check the top of the shock absorber mounts, behind the rear bulkhead.

A typical tool kit.

Spare wheel & tool kit   4 3 2 1
Is there a spare wheel? If so, what condition is it in and is it the correct wheel for the car? If fitted with alloys, you may find that the spare is a pressed steel version. The tyre may be worn or illegal.

Is there a tool kit? Does it appear to be complete? The original kit usually included, at the very least, a wheel bolt spanner, with a flat end to remove wheel trim/'knave plates', and a sparkplug spanner, all of which were stored in a plastic pouch with embossed Alfa Romeo logo.

The jack and tool kit housed in a recess in the boot of a 1982 US model.

Mechanicals
Under the bonnet (hood)   4 3 2 1
A clean and well-detailed engine bay is a very good indicator of what level of care the car has received. Is the bonnet stay present, and does it support the panel? Is the original 'recommended lubricant sticker' present on the underside of the bonnet (hood)? If missing, it's likely that the under-bonnet has been resprayed at some point.

Turn on the sidelights and check the function of the under-bonnet light. Heat from the engine tends to make these brittle and they soon break. Replacements are available.

Evidence of an owner's care in this engine bay.

Four engine sizes were offered in the Giulia range – see Chapter 17. Checking out the serial number is covered in Chapter 7. A lack of anti-freeze can cause a cracked cylinder block and/or cylinder head. The 2000 engine has thinner castings and is particularly prone to cracking. Cracks appear first around the oil pressure sensor and behind the carburettors/fuel-injection. Cracks in the cylinder head are most likely to show up around the sparkplug holes.

Head gasket problems are not uncommon due to differing thermal expansion rates between the aluminium block and steel wet liners, a problem evidenced by oil in the coolant, or

The lubricants sticker and under-bonnet light.

rapid coolant loss and steam from the exhaust. Regular maintenance, especially oil and filter changes, is the key to engine longevity, so service history is very important.

The fusebox on early versions was exposed to dirt, particularly if missing the cover.

Check the fan blades for damage, and look at the condition of the battery.

Wiring   ④ ③ ② ①

Does the wiring look as if it has been replaced? Check for soundness and good connections. Early models have the fuse box located in the engine bay, where it is exposed to moisture and dirt. Newer cars have the fuse box installed under the facia.

Radiator & fans   ④ ③ ② ①

With a cold engine look for stains or leaks. Run a finger along and under the radiator. Unscrew the radiator/expansion tank cap and check coolant level, looking for evidence of emulsified oil. Ask the owner when the anti-freeze/inhibitor was last checked; not only is it essential in winter it also guards against internal electrolytic corrosion. Right-hand drive converted cars often use Sud SC/ 33 expansion tanks re-located to the near side, which are prone to splitting. Check if any fan blades are broken or missing. The protective shroud is also often missing. Series 4 Spiders have two electric fans.

Hoses   ④ ③ ② ①

Check the tightness of the securing clips on all visible hoses. Run a finger around the circumference of each hose, feeling for signs of leakage or cracks. Check adjacent areas for anti-freeze/oil staining.

Battery   ④ ③ ② ①

Is the battery date marked? Does it fit tightly in its tray, indicating that it is the right size? A recent, strong, and healthy battery is important, as quite a kick is needed to start these cars, especially when they have not run for a while and the oil is thick. Are the battery fixings secure, and the connections tight and free of corrosion? Do the terminals appear to have been greased? Look alongside and around the base of the battery tray for localised corrosion. The boot mounted battery on Bosch injected cars is often neglected as it's hidden by a cover.

Brake & clutch master cylinders   ④ ③ ② ①

1600 Duettos had a mechanical clutch so no clutch master cylinder. Right-hand drive cars, with the bottom-hinged brake and clutch pedal, have both master cylinders located immediately under the floor, where protection from the elements is minimal so they are prone to damage. Replacements are usually available, but can be expensive. Left-hand drive cars

Brake and clutch master cylinders are poorly protected under the floor on RHD versions.

have under-bonnet mounted items. Look for leaks, low or dirty fluid and corroded pipework.

Brake servo

1600 Duettos are usually fitted with an aftermarket servo. Single servos were fitted to most other early models, and to the smallest engined versions. Twin servos were fitted to US cars from the 1750 Spider Veloce, and Euro and UK spec cars from the Kamm tail models

The twin brake servos on a RHD car.

Late Spider with brake servo incorporating master cylinder.

onwards. The systems are not identical. Other left-hand drive cars and later US cars have modern-style servos incorporating the brake master cylinder.

Washer system

Early cars had a foot pump. If it no longer works, it may be necessary to convert to an electric model or fit a used unit. Various types of reservoir were fitted. Series 4s' are located in the front left-hand wheelarch with a remote filler.

Engine leaks

Oil seeping from the exhaust side of the engine, beneath the manifold, indicates a problem: head gasket replacement may be necessary. Oil can drip down the front of the sump from a leaking crankshaft seal, which is a little messy, but not serious.

Engine mounts

Check for rocking when the engine is at a warm idle. Another indication of wear is excessive rocking of the gearlever when the engine is under load. Worn engine mounts are common, but replacement mounts and brackets are available and inexpensive.

Replacement engine mounts are inexpensive. (Courtesy E B Spares)

Air intake

The air filter on most Spiders is housed in a prominent cylinder on the right-hand side of the engine, with trunking extending to an air intake behind the radiator grille. The 1600 Duetto and 1750 long tailed Spiders have an inlet that crosses the cylinder head from the carburettors to a pancake filter on the opposite side.

The 'pancake' filter with crossover trunking fitted to long tail Spiders.

Early Spica injected cars have a flatter cylinder, marked

'Iniezione', which changed to a compact arrangement with the arrival of variable valve timing. Bosch injected cars have a square filter in a large container mounted low in the left-hand side of the engine bay. Check casings, hoses, and filters.

Dellorto carbs with the air filter removed for cleaning.

Bosch fuel injection – lots of hoses to check.

Carburettors & fuel injection

Carburettors may be Dellorto, Weber or Solex, depending upon the model and supply. All three have similar performance, but Solex is the least favoured as it wears with age and spare parts are unobtainable. The spindles become noisy, as they turn directly within the carburettor body, instead of within roller bearings like the others. A variable idle speed may be an indication of spindle wear.

Rubber carburettor mountings can harden and crack. If you suspect this, spray WD40 or similar on the carburettor mounts while the engine is running. Rising revs indicate a leak. Replacement mounts are obtainable, but expensive.

Carburettors require tuning by an expert, but once done they generally stay in tune. Rough running due to a dirty air filter is quite common and easily rectified. SPICA mechanical injection has a poor reputation, but, if carefully maintained by a specialist, can work well. Little is known about it outside the US. Many cars have been converted to carburettors. If so, is it legal in your state?

Bosch Motronic and Jetronic cars are reliable and need little maintenance, although slow driving can cause a build-up of carbon. Surging idle usually means a sticking idle air valve. Check the condition of the rubber intake sleeves, pipes and hoses. ECUs for Bosch injected cars are fitted inside, under the rear shelf.

Exhaust manifolds don't often give problems.

Exhaust manifold & down pipes

Not often a problem but look for signs of splits or cracks when the engine is idling. You can detect a loose manifold by listening for a 'blow' in that area.

Steering box

Steering box oil should be at the correct level and the box should not leak.

Steering box on early right-hand drive car. Note ribbed hose for scuttle drainage.

Front suspension & brakes ☐₄ ☐₃ ☐₂ ☐₁

The front suspension may creak, possibly due to worn bushes, which are not easy to replace. Apart from early Duettos, which were fitted with Dunlop disc brakes, all Spiders have the reliable ATE system.

Rear suspension & brakes ☐₄ ☐₃ ☐₂ ☐₁

Bushes wear out and rear spring life can be short, with the back of the car appearing to sag; neither is it uncommon for springs to break. The characteristic jiggling sensation over bumps will be worse if the cone bushes that locate the suspension are worn.

The webbing rebound straps for the live rear axle can snap, but can be replaced. If the seller tells you that the car is fitted with a handling kit, ask exactly what was done and who fitted the parts. A car fitted with new springs will tend to sit rather high until the springs settle. US spec cars generally have softer suspension settings.

The brake discs can become thin or rusty through lack of regular use, especially at the back where they tend to take less punishment. Look for scoring on the discs which may indicate severely worn pads. Some brake parts are difficult to source.

Rear axle ☐₄ ☐₃ ☐₂ ☐₁

Look for signs of oil leakage from the side seals or from the pinion. A limited slip differential – an option on the 1750 Spider – became standard on the 2000s. Series 4 rear axles are prone to wear.

Gearbox ☐₄ ☐₃ ☐₂ ☐₁

You'll be checking the function of the gearbox on the test drive, so, for now, just check for any sign of leaking oil.

Test drive (not less than 15 minutes)

Ideally, this should be over a variety of roads. Spiders do not exhibit their true driving qualities in urban traffic, and unless you are able to find some open road, you're unlikely to get the feel of the car.

Adjust the seat, and become acquainted with the controls before setting off. Floor mounted pedals take a bit of getting used to and can be off-putting at first. Pendant pedal cars feel quite straightforward.

Most cars are now fitted with at least one door mirror, and you will need these if the hood is up. Adjust rear view mirrors to your liking. Electric mirror adjusters are located on the transmission tunnel console. Check you're able to judge where the front of the car is before moving off.

Front suspension bushes may be worn. Note spring pans.

Scored disc may indicate worn brake pads.

Look for leaks from differential. Prop shaft and exhaust have been removed here.

Cold start 4 3 2 1

Spiders fitted with carburettors can be difficult to start, and discovering the best method with a particular car is really a case of trial and error. Some owners prefer not to use the choke, but prime the carburettors by pumping the accelerator a few times before turning the key. Others will use the choke and a light throttle until the engine fires. It helps if you depress the clutch at the same time. The choke can be returned as soon as the engine runs cleanly, and the revs can be maintained for a short time on the hand throttle. Disengage this when under way. Repeated, unsuccessful attempts to start the car may flatten the battery, so if the engine fails to fire after a couple of turns, leave it for a moment before trying again. Warm the engine a little before setting off. SPICA injected cars should have the accelerator depressed halfway and may cough a few times, running unevenly until warm. If the fuel pressure warning light doesn't go out soon after the ignition is switched on, this will indicate injection problems. Poor maintenance is usually the cause. Bosch injected cars should start readily with no throttle applied and with clutch disengaged. Check that the starter motor is not noisy and that it disengages rapidly.

Warm start 4 3 2 1

Carburettored cars can be equally difficult to start when warm and, again, procedures vary from one example to another, although turning the key with the throttle fully depressed for a moment usually works. Take your foot off as soon as the engine fires. Be careful not to flood the carburettors by repeatedly attempting this approach. If the engine does not start first time, Bosch injected cars should have the accelerator pedal depressed slightly for subsequent attempts.

Handbrake (parking brake) 4 3 2 1

This is easy to locate on the transmission tunnel, and should be able to hold the car on a slope. It may be necessary to pull up the lever quite firmly.

Warning lights (telltales) 4 3 2 1

A warning light appears when the handbrake is engaged; check that it has gone out before driving off as it's not uncommon for the handbrake to not fully release. Other warning lights are for main beam, side/headlight, heater fan, indicators, low oil pressure/choke, and alternator. Later cars have lights for hazard flashers, fog lamps and minimum brake fluid. Some US cars have a 'fasten seat belt' warning. Most versions also have a low fuel warning indicator.

Clutch 4 3 2 1

Clutches tend to have relatively short lives, and can suffer from harsh treatment, in which case they may slip. Listen for a noisy thrust release bearing.

Gearbox (transmission) 4 3 2 1

The gearlever (shiftlever) may seem oddly placed, but once under way will fall readily to hand. It has a long throw, and the action should be quite precise. The synchromesh on second gear is often weak, causing a crunch when changing down unless coaxed into place. Proceed with care until the gearbox oil has warmed thoroughly. An effective way to obviate worn synchros is to double de-clutch when down-changing. With practice this can be a satisfying driving technique.

If the 'box jumps out of gear, especially when reversing, the rather weak selector forks could be bending. Does the gearbox sound noisy on the move? Test for a change in transmission noise when the clutch is depressed. Some specialists recommend reconditioning your existing gearbox rather than exchanging it for a rebuilt example which may have unknown faults. From 1991 a ZF 3-speed automatic transmission, which does little for the car, was offered in the US.

Steering
4 3 2 1

The steering should feel light and responsive when under way; one of the pleasures of driving a Spider. It may feel heavy at slow speeds, particularly if the steering wheel is of smaller diameter than the original, or wider-than-standard wheels and tyres have been fitted. This heaviness occurs on Series 3s fitted with 60 profile tires. Wide wheels and tyres may improve grip, but will do so at the expense of steering feel. Steering vibration is usually due to wheels which require balancing. Series 4s have nicely weighted ZF power steering

Brakes
4 3 2 1

The four-wheel disc brakes are reassuring in action but require more pressure than a modern car. A 'graunching' noise when applying the brakes could indicate worn pads, or rust on the surface of the discs, particularly if the car has stood for a while. Occasionally, the brake pads can stick in the callipers due to a build-up of dust and dirt: this can lead to binding or pulling to one side. Binding and a hard-to-depress brake pedal can also be caused by a failing brake master cylinder.

Brakes that feel spongy may need bleeding. Apply the brakes fairly hard, when it is safe to do so, and check that the car pulls up straight and true.

Noise & vibration
4 3 2 1

A rumbling sound from under the car could be from worn bearings in the propeller (drive) shaft. A droning sound from the rear of the car may come from a worn differential, or from a differential running with insufficient oil. A helicopter-like 'whooping' sound may indicate wheel bearing problems. Does the engine run smoothly without undue noise? Are the big ends knocking? It's easy to become paranoid about noises, especially in an older car, but be alert to anything that doesn't sound quite right.

Vibration may be caused by an out-of-balance propeller shaft, or worn doughnuts.

Performance
4 3 2 1

A Spider with carburettors should respond quickly to throttle input, and become brisk and lively when up to temperature. It will be necessary to keep the revs up on the smaller engined variants, but all are sweet and eager to be taken up toward the red line. The 1750 Spider is often considered the smoothest of all, and although the 2000 develops a little more power, it's harsher. US spec cars with clean air equipment have less power and are not as lively. The 1974 model is the most powerful SPICA injected car. Bosch injected cars have better throttle response and driveability characteristics. Series 4s with Bosch Motronic and VVT feel less responsive below 4000rpm. Catalyst fitted cars (standard in the EEC from 1993) are down in power by 6bhp. These later cars, however, cruise well with less fuss and noise.

Have you spotted signs of exhaust smoke in the rear view mirrors during your drive? A puff of smoke on the overrun when lifting your foot off the throttle may be a sign of worn valve seats. These wear with age, and replacement is relatively straightforward. Constant exhaust smoke could be indicative of more serious engine problems.

Instruments
These are clear and easy to read. Check that they all function when on the move.

Oil pressure
Oil pressure gauges and sensors can be of poor quality, and are not always accurate. The needle should rise quickly when the engine is started, and remain fairly constant as the revs increase and decrease. With a hot engine, the reading should be a minimum of 7psi at idle, and 50-70psi when running fast.

Water temperature
Engine temperature should rise quite quickly, and settle at just under the halfway point when fully warm, around 81-85°C.

Switches
Check the operation of each switch in turn. With some right-hand drive models, when fifth gear is engaged the gear knob may be very near to the indicator stalks. Check that the heater/demister/air conditioning are operational.

After your test drive
Before you turn off the engine, engage the handbrake and get out of the car to walk around the back to check for exhaust smoke. After you've turned off the engine, wipe your finger around the inside of the exhaust pipe. Black, sooty residue can indicate that the engine has been burning oil, whilst an excessively rich mixture will point to worn or badly tuned carburettors.

Ramp check
Examination of the underside of the car will only be possible using a ramp, hoist or a pit. Most exhaust and tyre centres will let you put a car on their ramp for five minutes or so when they're not particularly busy. The best solution is to take the car to a vehicle testing (MoT in the UK) station, where the examiner may allow you to join him for a step-by-step examination.

Begin your examination at the front valance and methodically work your way backward. As you inspect the underside of the car, keep in mind that every crevice is a potential trap for mud and damp.

Ramp check (rust-proofing)

☑ ☑ ☑ ☑

A well cared for car will be clean, and will have received regular rust-proofing to the wheelarches and on the underside with a reputable product such as Waxoyl. There should, at the very least, be some evidence of anti-corrosion protection. As you check the car from underneath, make sure that the cavity wax has not blocked the drain holes. If an underseal has been applied, look for signs of lifting, which could promote corrosion. If the car is caked in mud and road dirt, then you have a problem. You could use a screwdriver to prise away the mud at various points, but you'd be better off telling the vendor that you're not interested in looking any further until the car has been steam cleaned!

Ramp check (front valance and crossmember)

☑ ☑ ☑ ☑

Check the condition of the front valance and the location points for the front anti-roll bar. The front crossmember under the radiator can corrode, especially if the radiator has leaked at some time. View this area from the side, forward of the front wheel. Replacement box section front crossmembers are available, but don't ignore any corrosion present.

The front crossmember under the radiator and the roll bar mounting. Aftermarket sump guard fitted here.

Ramp check (splashguards & 'A' post area)

☑ ☑ ☑ ☑

With the car on a ramp, a more detailed examination of this critical area can be made. As mentioned, the front splashguard is often corroded or missing, as is the rear one which is designed to protect the base of the 'A' post, sills (rockers), wings (fenders), and front bulkhead. A regular clean out and protection from rust is essential, so make a thorough examination of the nooks and ledges. Ideally, ask if you can remove the splashguards, which may be possible if they are secured with screws. Repairs here are difficult and expensive, especially if poorly carried out in the past. Series 4 Spiders have full arch liners, which should be in good condition and completely sealed.

The splashguards are designed to protect this area, ahead of the front wheels.

Ramp check (crossmember & inner wing area)

☑ ☑ ☑ ☑

Look at the area where the crossmember under the engine joins the inner wings. Are there signs of accident damage or corrosion? Ask the vendor to sit in the car and gently turn the steering wheel from side-to-side whilst you look at the joins. It should also be possible to see the mounting points for the steering box and idler arm through the inner wheelarches, which can crack due to heavy steering loads.

Check for corrosion here and around the front suspension mounting points/turrets.

Ramp check (sills/rockers) 4 3 2 1

Use of the ramp will enable a closer examination of these

Check that sill drain holes are clear.

critical areas, so check the entire length between front and rear wheels. Look for bodged repairs, holes, and signs of corrosion. Probe with your screwdriver and use your magnet to detect filler. Check drain holes are present and free from blockage, including those in the adjoining rear wings. A better assessment of Series3QV/4s can be made from this angle

Engine crossmember between sump and gearbox.

Ramp check (jacking points) 4 3 2 1

Examine the front and rear jacking points, which are prone to corrosion and should not be relied upon to support the car.

Ramp check (spring pans, master cylinders & pipework) 4 3 2 1

In extreme cases, the spring pans at the base of the springs can rot through, causing an alarming collapse of the front suspension. Rust can gain a hold on the inside of the pan if the drain holes are blocked, or on the outside if the car has been kept in the damp for long periods. Pans can be replaced, but specialist tools are required as this can be a dangerous job. On cars with floor mounted clutch and brake pedals, the respective master cylinders will be found immediately under the foot well, 'protected' by an ineffective weather guard.

Sill, with jacking point just above trailing arm mounting.

Examine all the pipework for the brake, clutch and fuel lines, where visible.

Front suspension spring pans and steering linkage.

Ramp check (foot wells) 4 3 2 1

Check the foot wells from the underside. If you were unable to check the rear drain holes from inside, do so now. Check that any welded patches have been seam sealed.

Underfloor mounted cylinders, shown here without weatherguards.

Ramp check (trailing arm attachment points) 4 3 2 1

Check where the rear suspension trailing arms attach to the underside, as well as the arms themselves. As mentioned, this is a vital area – and corrosion here may mean that the car is beyond saving. Examine the area around the shock absorber mounts.

Ramp check (exhaust system)   4 3 2 1

The exhaust system has three silencer boxes. Complete exhausts – including stainless steel systems – are readily available. The shape of the system varies from model-to-model, and problems can occur if the wrong type is installed. Establish that the exhaust has been hung properly so that the bracketing and rubber mountings allow the exhaust to rock from side-to-side a little or splitting may otherwise occur. While the engine is running, look for signs of leakage. Only an emissions test will indicate the condition of a catalyst. These have good durability.

Check that the exhaust system is sound.

Ramp check (rear axle area)   4 3 2 1

Comprehensively check out the propeller shaft for play, worn mountings/doughnuts. Look for oil leaks around the differential. Check the condition of the webbing rebound straps for the live rear axle; feeble-looking, broken or missing loops especially. Replacement is straightforward. The rear suspension bump stops are rubber blocks which can break away, so check that they are present. It should also be possible to gain an impression of the condition of the suspension bushes.

Webbing strap and bump rubber on rear suspension (arrowed).

Ramp check (spare wheel well & fuel tank)   4 3 2 1

The spare wheel well and fuel tank can both be examined carefully from underneath. Check for rusting and tank leakage.

Ramp check (rear valance)   4 3 2 1

Check the bottom of the rear valance below the bumper, which is another area very prone to rust. Although replacements can be found, they are expensive to buy and have fitted. Generally check drain holes and examine the area behind the plastic bumpers on S3 & S4 cars.

Examine fuel tank and spare wheel well, either side of exhaust silencer.

Evaluation procedure

Add up the total points score: **316 = excellent, possibly concours; 237 = good; 158 = average; 79 = poor.** Cars scoring over 221 will be completely useable and will require only maintenance and care to keep in condition. Cars scoring between 79 and 161 will require full restoration (at much the same cost). Cars scoring between 162 and 220 will require very careful assessment of necessary repair/restoration costs in order to reach a realistic value.

10 Auctions
– sold! Another way to buy your dream

Pros: Prices will usually be lower than those of dealers or private sellers, and you might grab a real bargain on the day. Auctioneers have usually established clear title with the seller. At the venue you can usually examine documentation relating to the vehicle.

Cons: You have to rely on a sketchy catalogue description of condition and history. The opportunity to inspect is limited, and you cannot drive the car. Auction cars are often a little below par and may require some work. It's easy to overbid. There will usually be a buyer's premium to pay in addition to the auction hammer price.

Which auction?

Auctions by established auctioneers are advertised in car magazines and on the auction houses' websites. A catalogue, or a simple printed list of the lots for auctions, might only be available a day or two ahead, though often lots are listed and pictured on auctioneers' websites much earlier. Contact the auction company to ask if previous auction selling prices are available as this is useful information (details of past sales are often available on websites).

Catalogue, entry fee and payment details

When you purchase the catalogue of the vehicles in the auction, it often acts as a ticket, allowing two people to attend the viewing days and the auction. Catalogue details tend to be comparatively brief, but will include information such as 'one owner from new, low mileage, full service history', etc. It will also usually show a guide price to give you some idea of what to expect to pay and will tell you what is charged as a 'Buyer's premium'. The catalogue will also contain details of acceptable forms of payment. At the fall of the hammer an immediate deposit is usually required, the balance payable within 24 hours. If the plan is to pay by cash there may be a cash limit. Some auctions will accept payment by debit card. Sometimes credit or charge cards are acceptable, but will often incur a charge. A bank draft or bank transfer will have to be arranged in advance with your bank as well as with the auction house. No car will be released before **all** payments are cleared. If delays occur in payment transfers then storage costs can accrue.

Buyer's premium

A buyer's premium will be added to the hammer price: don't forget this in your calculations. It is not unusual for there to be a further state tax or local tax on the purchase price and/or on the buyer's premium.

Viewing

In some instances it's possible to view on the day, or days before, as well as in the hours prior to the auction. Auction officials are available to help out by opening engine and luggage compartments and to allow you to inspect the interior. Whilst the officials may start the engine for you, a test drive is out of the question. Crawling under and around the car as much as you want is permitted, but you can't suggest that the car you are interested in be jacked up, or attempt to do the job yourself. You can ask to see any available documentation.

Bidding

Before you take part in the auction, **decide your maximum bid – and then stick to it!**

It may take a while for the auctioneer to reach the lot you are interested in, so use that time to observe how other bidders behave. When it's the turn of your car, attract the auctioneer's attention and make an early bid. The auctioneer will then look to you for a reaction every time another bid is made. Usually the bids will be in fixed increments until bidding slows, when smaller increments will often be accepted before the hammer falls. If you want to withdraw from the bidding, make sure the auctioneer understands your intentions – a vigorous shake of the head when he or she looks to you for the next bid should do the trick!

Assuming that you are the successful bidder, the auctioneer will note your card or paddle number, and from that moment on you will be responsible for the vehicle.

If the car is unsold, either because it failed to reach the reserve or because there was little interest, it may be possible to negotiate with the owner, via the auctioneer, after the sale is over.

Successful bid

There are two more items to think about. How to get the car home, and insurance. If you can't drive the car, your own or a hired trailer is one way; another is to have the vehicle shipped using the facilities of a local company. The auction house will also have details of companies specialising in the transfer of cars.

Insurance for immediate cover can usually be purchased on site, but it may be more cost-effective to make arrangements with your own insurance company in advance, and then call to confirm the full details.

eBay & other online auctions?

eBay & other online auctions could land you a car at a bargain price, though you'd be foolhardy to bid without examining the car first, something most vendors encourage. A useful feature of eBay is that the geographical location of the car is shown, so you can narrow your choices to those within a realistic radius of home. Be prepared to be outbid in the last few moments of the auction. Remember that your bid is binding and it will be very, very difficult to get restitution in the case of a crooked vendor fleecing you – ***caveat emptor!***

Be aware that some cars offered for sale in online auctions are 'ghost' cars. Don't part with any cash without being sure that the vehicle does actually exist and is as described (usually pre-bidding inspection is possible).

Auctioneers

Barrett-Jackson www.barrett-jackson.com
Bonhams www.bonhams.com
British Car Auctions BCA) www.bca-europe.com or www.british-car-auctions.co.uk

Christies www.christies.com
Coys www.coys.co.uk
eBay www.ebay.com
H&H www.handh.co.uk
RM Sotheby's www.rmsothebys.com
Shannons www.shannons.com.au
Silver www.silverauctions.com

11 Paperwork
– correct documentation is essential

The paper trail

Classic, collector and prestige cars usually come with a large portfolio of paperwork, which has been accumulated and passed on by a succession of proud owners. This documentation represents the real history of the car and from it can be deduced the level of care the car has received, how much it's been used, which specialists have worked on it, and the dates of major repairs and restorations. All of this information will be priceless to you as the new owner, so be very wary of cars with little paperwork to support their claimed history.

Registration documents

All countries/states have some form of registration for private vehicles whether it's like the American 'pink slip' system or the British 'log book' system.

It is essential to check that the registration document is genuine, that it relates to the car in question, and that all the vehicle's details are correctly recorded, including chassis/VIN and engine numbers (if these are shown). If you are buying from the previous owner, his or her name and address will be recorded in the document: this will not be the case if you are buying from a dealer.

In the UK the current (Euro-aligned) registration document is named 'V5C,' and is printed in coloured sections of blue, green and pink. The blue section relates to the car specification, the green section has details of the new owner and the pink section is sent to the DVLA in the UK when the car is sold. A small section in yellow deals with selling the car within the motor trade.In the UK the DVLA will provide details of earlier keepers of the vehicle upon payment of a small fee, and much can be learned in this way.

If the car has a foreign registration there may be expensive and time-consuming formalities to complete. Do you really want the hassle?

Roadworthiness certificate

Most country/state administrations require that vehicles are regularly tested to prove that they are safe to use on the public highway and do not produce excessive emissions. In the UK that test (the 'MOT') is carried out at approved testing stations, for a fee. In the USA the requirement varies, but most states insist on an emissions test every two years as a minimum, while the police are charged with pulling over unsafe-looking vehicles.

In the UK the test is required on an annual basis once a vehicle becomes three years old. Of particular relevance for older cars is that the certificate issued includes the mileage reading recorded at the test date and, therefore, becomes an independent record of that car's history. Ask the seller if previous certificates are available. Without an MOT the vehicle should be trailered to its new home, unless you insist that a valid MOT is part of the deal. (Not such a bad idea this, as at least you will know the car was roadworthy on the day it was tested and you don't need to wait for the old certificate to expire before having the test done.)

In the UK, vehicles over 40 years old on May 20th each year, are exempt from MOT testing. Owners can still have the test carried out if they so wish.

Road license

The administration of every country/state charges some kind of tax for the use of its road system, the actual form of the 'road licence' and, how it is displayed, varying enormously country to country and state to state.

Whatever the form of the road licence, it must relate to the vehicle carrying it and must be present and valid if the car is to be driven on the public highway legally.

Changed legislation in the UK means that the seller of a car must surrender any existing road fund licence, and it is the responsibility of the new owner to re-tax the vehicle at the time of purchase and before the car can be driven on the road. It's therefore vital to see the Vehicle Registration Certificate (V5C) at the time of purchase, and to have access to the New Keeper Supplement (V5C/2), allowing the buyer to obtain road tax immediately.

In the UK, classic vehicles 40 years old or more on the 1st January each year get free road tax. It is still necessary to renew the tax status every year, even if there is no change.

If the car is untaxed because it has not been used for a period of time, the owner has to inform the licensing authorities.

Certificates of authenticity

For many makes of collectible car it is possible to get a certificate proving the age and authenticity (eg: engine and chassis numbers, paint colour and trim) of a particular vehicle. These are sometimes called 'Heritage Certificates' and if the car comes with one of these this is a definite bonus. If you want to obtain one, the relevant Owner's Club is the best starting point.

If the car has been used in European classic car rallies it may have a FIVA (Federation Internationale des Vehicules Anciens) certificate. The so-called 'FIVA Passport', or 'FIVA Vehicle Identity Card,' enables organisers and participants to recognise whether or not a particular vehicle is suitable for individual events. If you want to obtain such a certificate go to <www.fbhvc.co.uk> or <www.fiva.org>; similar organisations will exist in other countries, too.

Valuation certificate

Hopefully, the vendor will have a recent valuation certificate, or letter signed by a recognised expert stating how much he, or she, believes the particular car to be worth (such documents, together with photos, are usually necessary for 'agreed value' insurance). Generally, such documents should act only as confirmation of your own assessment of the car rather than a guarantee of value, as the expert has probably not seen the car in the flesh. The easiest way to find out how to obtain a formal valuation is to contact the Owner's Club.

Service history

Often these cars will have been serviced at home by enthusiastic (and hopefully capable) owners for a good number of years. Nevertheless, try to obtain as much service history and other paperwork pertaining to the car as you can. Naturally, dealer stamps, or specialist garage receipts score most points in the value stakes. However, anything helps in the great authenticity game, items like the original bill of sale, handbook, parts invoices and repair bills all adding to the story and character of the car. Even a brochure correct to the year of the car's manufacture is a useful document and something you may well have to search hard to locate in future years. If the seller claims that the car has been restored, then expect receipts and other evidence from a specialist restorer.

If the seller claims to have carried out regular servicing, ask what work was completed, when, and seek some evidence of it being done. Your assessment of the car's overall condition should tell you whether the seller's claims are genuine.

Restoration photographs

If the seller tells you that the car has been restored, expect to be shown a series of photographs taken while the restoration was under way. Pictures taken at various stages, and from various angles, should help you gauge the thoroughness of the work. If you buy the car, ask if you can have all the photographs as they form an important part of the vehicle's history. It's surprising how many sellers are happy to part with their car and accept your cash, but want to hang on to their photographs! In the latter event, you may be able to persuade the vendor to get a set of copies made.

Photographs taken during restoration can help you assess the thoroughness of the work. (Courtesy Stuart Braley)

12 What's it worth?
– let your head rule your heart

Condition

If the car you've been looking at is really bad, then you've probably not bothered to use the marking system in Chapter 9. You may not have even got as far as using that chapter at all!

If you did use the marking system you'll know whether the car is in Excellent (maybe concours), Good, Average or Poor condition or, perhaps, somewhere in-between these categories.

Many classic/collector car magazines run a regular price guide. If you haven't bought the latest issues, do so now and compare their suggested values for the model you are thinking of buying: also look at the auction prices they're reporting. Values have been fairly stable for some time, but some models will always be more sought-after than others. Trends can change too. The values published in the magazines tend to vary from one to another, as do their scales of condition, so read carefully the guidance notes they provide. Bear in mind that a car which is truly a recent show winner could be worth more than the highest scale published. Assuming that the car you have in mind is not in show/concours condition, relate the level of condition that you judge the car to be in to the appropriate guide price. How does the figure compare with the asking price? Before you start haggling with the seller, consider what affect any variation from standard specification might have on the car's value.

If you are buying from a dealer, remember the price will carry a dealer's premium.

Desirable options/extras

The range of factory fitted options tended to vary from market-to-market. Spiders sold in the USA usually had a comprehensive specification, with air conditioning, electric windows and electric mirrors sometimes available. Later Spiders could be specified with leather upholstery; usually more durable than its cheaper counterpart. Tonneau and hood covers are a useful addition if you make full use of the soft top, as are aftermarket rear 'draught screens'.

A factory hard top was offered with each successive model. Many are rare and sought-after. The Series 3 & 4 Spiders had a comprehensive 3-window design, with a headlining, interior light and heated rear window. Early finned alloy wheels look good when new, but deteriorate quickly. Those fitted to later cars are more durable. A set of period alloys of sympathetic style will enhance a Spider's appearance, as will a suitable wood or leather rimmed steering wheel and gearlever knob. Nardi or Momo items are desirable. Tuning and handling kits, designed for the Spider, can enhance driveability, and electronic ignition can aid starting and smooth running.

Undesirable extras

Unless you intend to use your Spider for track days or competition, extreme tuning and handling modifications – which may improve horsepower and grip – often do little for driveability. Sometimes fitted to S3 & S4 cars, unsympathetic alloy wheels with ultra low profile tyres can ruin the ride and do little for scuttle shake. Smaller than standard steering wheels make slow driving tedious. Decals applied to limited edition US models or two-tone paint schemes can be a matter of personal taste. Extreme sound systems take up lots of space and are of little value in a soft top car.

In the UK many Spiders have been imported and sold with left-hand drive. This has become less of a problem to deal with in recent years, and comes down to personal choice, though will have a negative effect on value.

Striking a deal
Negotiate on the basis of your condition assessment, mileage, and fault rectification cost. Also take into account the car's specification. Be realistic about the value, but don't be completely intractable: a small compromise on the part of the vendor or buyer will often facilitate a deal at little real cost.

Former Alfa Romeo Grand Prix driver Bruno Giacomelli likes Spiders so much that he recently bought back the actual US spec S2 Spider Veloce he first owned in 1980! (Courtesy Bruno Giacomelli)

13 Do you really want to restore?
– it'll take longer, and cost more than you think ...

So you've seen a Spider that looks like it needs just a little work, or another that obviously requires a full restoration. The frightening thing is that the cost of restoring either of these could work out to be much the same – especially if you're

Full restoration of sills is often essential to any restoration project. (Courtesy Stuart Braley)

paying someone to do the work. Labour will be the biggest cost in any restoration and hourly rates can vary enormously.

Fortunately, there are a number of knowledgeable, enthusiastic specialists who enjoy working on and being involved with older Alfa Romeos – but they still need to make a living. Some of these may have worked for an Alfa Romeo dealer and now prefer to run their own business, often in less salubrious surroundings with lower overheads. Owner's Clubs and other enthusiasts can put you in touch with a specialist in your area, usually with a personal recommendation. It's worth discussing your needs with an expert before buying a car that needs

A rare long tail Spider, but would you want to take it on?

work. Some restorers will assess the car and give you an estimate, whilst others might prefer to start the work and log their hours. Either way, the total cost could work out to be much more than you bargained for. If you do instruct a restorer the important thing is to visit him regularly to gauge progress, the quality of work, and perhaps take photographs on each visit. It is essential that you keep an eye on costs and agree payment terms in advance. Many restorers will ask for stage payments as work proceeds and may stop work on your car

The three sill panels are the key to structural integrity. Replacements are shown here.

until paid. Some may ask you to pay for or to supply parts.

If you think you have the ability, facilities, dedication, and time to tackle the job yourself, be sure to properly assess the task you're taking on. Unfinished restoration projects can be found in any classic car 'for sale' section. Ask yourself why they gave up? Did they lose interest, run out of money – or patience? Could you take over such a project or take one on in the first place and honestly believe that you could complete the job? Might it be viable for you to do some of the work and pay a professional to do the difficult bits? Some specialists prefer to complete a project, rather than working around someone who may not have matching skills. Another option

A lot of work has gone into getting the car to this stage. (Courtesy Stuart Braley)

might be to buy a roadworthy car with a view to undertaking a rolling restoration, but this may cost more in the long term.

Mechanical work will almost certainly be less expensive than bodywork restoration.

If the car is really poor and you intend a full 'nut and bolt' restoration it's often best to buy the worst car you can find, so long as the vital structural parts and irreplaceable components are salvageable. A full restoration can take a long time – even if you give the work to a professional – so ask yourself if you can wait that long before driving off in your pristine Spider.

Unless you really are sure that you want to embark upon a restoration, either by a professional or yourself, it would probably be cheaper to seek out a really good car and be prepared to pay a fair price for it. The choice is yours ...

14 Paint problems
– bad complexion, including dimples, pimples and bubbles

Paint faults generally occur due to lack of protection/maintenance, or poor preparation prior to a respray or touch-up. Some of the following conditions may be present in the car you're looking at:

Orange peel

This appears as an uneven paint surface, similar in appearance to the skin of an orange. The fault is caused by the failure of atomized paint droplets to flow into each other when they hit the surface. It's sometimes possible to rub out the effect with proprietary paint cutting/ rubbing compound or very fine grades of abrasive paper. A respray may be necessary in severe cases. Consult a

Orange peel.

bodywork repairer/paint shop for advice on the particular car.

Cracking

Severe cases are likely to have been caused by too heavy an application of paint (or filler beneath the paint). Also, insufficient stirring of the paint before application can result in the components being improperly mixed, and cracking can result. Incompatibility with the paint already on the panel can have a similar effect. To rectify the problem it is necessary to rub down to a smooth, sound finish before respraying the problem area.

Crazing

Sometimes the paint takes on a crazed rather than a cracked appearance when the problems mentioned under 'Cracking' are present. This problem can also be caused by a reaction between the underlying surface and the paint. Paint removal and respraying the problem area is usually the only solution.

Blistering

Almost always caused by corrosion of the metal beneath the paint. Usually perforation will be found in the metal and the damage will usually be worse than that suggested by the area of blistering. The metal will have to be repaired before repainting.

Rust blistering ...

Micro blistering
Usually the result of an economy respray where inadequate heating has allowed moisture to settle on the car before spraying. Consult a paint specialist, but usually damaged paint will have to be removed before partial or full respraying. Can also be caused by car covers that don't 'breathe'.

Fading
Some colours, especially reds, are prone to fading if subjected to strong sunlight for long periods without the benefit of polish protection. Sometimes proprietary paint restorers and/or paint cutting/rubbing compounds will retrieve the situation. Often a respray is the only real solution.

Peeling
Often a problem with metallic paintwork when the sealing laquer becomes damaged and begins to peel off. Poorly applied paint may also peel. The remedy is to strip and start again!

Dimples
Dimples in the paintwork are caused by the residue of polish (particularly silicone types) not being removed properly before respraying. Paint removal and repainting is the only solution.

Dents
Small dents are usually easily cured by the 'Dentmaster', or equivalent process, that sucks or pushes out the dent (as long as the paint surface is still intact). Companies offering dent removal services usually come to your home: consult your telephone directory.

Dimples and orange peel.

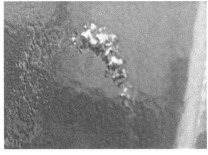
Reaction and rust blistering.

15 Problems due to lack of use

– just like their owners, cars need exercise!

Cars, like humans, are at their most efficient if they exercise regularly. A run of at least ten miles, once a week, is recommended for classics.

Seized components

Pistons in calipers, slave and master cylinders can seize.

The clutch may seize if the plate becomes stuck to the flywheel because of corrosion.

Handbrakes (parking brakes) can seize if the cables and linkages rust.

Pistons can seize in the bores due to corrosion.

Fluids

Old, acidic oil can corrode bearings.

Uninhibited coolant can corrode internal waterways. Lack of anti-freeze can cause core plugs to be pushed out, and even cracks in the block or head. Silt settling and solidifying can cause overheating.

Brake fluid absorbs water from the atmosphere and should be renewed every two years. Old fluid with a high water content can cause corrosion and pistons/calipers to seize (freeze), and can cause brake failure when the water turns to vapour near hot braking components,

Tyre problems

Tyres which have borne the weight of the car in a single position for some time will develop flat spots, resulting in some (usually temporary) vibration. The tyre walls may have cracks or (blister-type) bulges, meaning new tyres are needed.

Shock absorbers (dampers)

With lack of use, the dampers will lose their elasticity or even seize. Creaking, groaning and stiff suspension are signs of this problem.

Rubber and plastic

Radiator hoses may have perished and split, possibly resulting in the loss of all coolant. Window and door seals can harden and leak. Gaitors/boots can crack. Wiper blades will harden.

Suspension components can seize and tyres deteriorate.

Electrics

The battery will be of little use if it has not been charged for many months.

Earthing/grounding problems are common when the connections have corroded.

Old bullet and spade type electrical connectors commonly rust/corrode and will need disconnecting, cleaning and protection (eg: Vaseline).

Sparkplug electrodes will often have corroded in an unused engine.

Wiring insulation can harden and fail.

Rotting exhaust system

Exhaust gas contains a high water content so exhaust systems corrode very quickly from the inside when the car is not used.

Hoods/folding soft top

If a car is stored or the hard top put on with the hood/soft top folded and damp, it will rot.

Unwelcome visitors

A Spider makes a comfortable home for a full range of rodents, insects and other animals. These can do untold damage to wiring, upholstery and trim.

Check if the car you are keen on has been in regular use.

– key people, organisations and companies in the Spider world

Clubs

Alfa Romeo Owners Club UK
Tel: 07753 857029
www.aroc-uk.com

AROC 105/115 Giulia Register – UK
Stuart Taylor – Registrar
Tel: 07808 720450
Email: 105register@aroc-uk.com
www.aroc-uk.com/105register

AROC USA
www.aroc.usa.org

S.C.A.R.B.
(AROC of The Netherlands)
www.alfaclub.nl

Parts

Contact clubs or use the web to find specialists in your country.

Alfaholics
Tel: 01275 349449
www.alfaholics.com

Alfa Workshop (Jamie Porter)
01763 244441
www.alfaworkshop.co.uk

ClassicAlfa
Richard Norris
Tel: 020 8693 0707
www.classicalfa.com

EB Spares Ltd
Westbury,
Wiltshire
Tel: 01373 823856

www.ebspares.co.uk

Restorations/Service/Sales

Contact clubs or use the web to find specialists in your country.

Alfa Workshop (Jamie Porter)
01763 244441
www.alfaworkshop.co.uk

Automeo
Bristol
Les Dufty Tel: 07802 364445
www.automeo.co.uk

Black & White Garage
Tel: 01635 200444
www.bwgarage.com

BLS Automotive – Lincoln
Tel: 01522 531529
www.blsautomotive.co.uk

T A & J M Coburn
Full interior trim
Tel: 01793 721501
www.coburnhoods.co.uk

John Williams Classics
Tel:07967 203007
www.johnwilliamsclassiccars.com

Lombarda Carriage Co (1964) Ltd
www.alfaromeolombarda.co.uk

MGS Coachworks
Mike Spenceley
Tel: 020 8645 0555

Peak Alfa
Hope Valley, Peak District
Roger Evans
Tel: 01433 623050

Sunnyside Garage
Dagenham
Tel: 0208 599 3484

Veloce Sport
01529 469035
www.velocesport.co.uk

Willow Body Repairs (Roger Dykes)
Hall Farm, Great Bricett, Ipswich, Suffolk
IP7 7DN
Tel: 07717015126 / 07899318780
willowscbr@gmail.com

Other websites

alfaowner.com
www.alfaowner.com

AROC of Australia
www.alfaclub.org.au

AROC of New Zealand
www.arocnz.org.nz

Books

Alfa Romeo 105 Series Spider, The Complete Story, Jim Talbott & Andrew Brown, Crowood, ISBN: 978 1 78500 649 4
Alfa Romeo Giulia GT Coupé Essential Buyer's Guide by Keith Booker, Veloce Publishing Ltd, ISBN: 1 904788 69 6
Alfa Romeo Giulia Coupé GT & GTA Enlarged 2nd Edition by John Tipler, Veloce Publishing, ISBN: 1 903706 47 5
Alfa Romeo Tipo 33: race & individual chassis history by Ed McDonough & Peter Collins, Veloce Publishing Ltd, ISBN: 1 904788 71 8
Alfa Romeo Duetto Spider – Giorgio Nada Editore, ISBN: 88 7911 063 2
Alfa Romeo Giulia Spiders and Coupés by Richard Bremner, MRP
ISBN: 0 947981 59 4
Alfa Romeo Spider 1966-87, Brooklands Books, ISBN: 1 869826 477
Alfa Romeo Spider 1966-91 Gold Portfolio Brooklands Books
ISBN: 1 85520 1364
Alfa Romeo Giulia History & Restoration by Pat Braden, MBI
ISBN: 0 87938 529 4
Autobooks Giulia Workshop Manual 1962-78, ISBN: 0 85146 128 X
Original Alfa Romeo Spider by Chris Rees, Bay View Book
ISBN: 0 76031162 5
Alfa Romeo Spider – The Complete Story by John Tipler, Crowood
ISBN: 1 86126 1225
Illustrated Alfa Romeo Buyer's Guide by Joe Benson, MBI, ISBN: 0 87938 633 9

Various parts catalogues, handbooks and manuals available from parts specialists.

17 Vital statistics
– essential data at your fingertips

Although Spider production encompassed 28 years, the basic specification of the original 1600 Duetto remained intact throughout this period. There were many refinements and four different engine sizes. The most significant change took place in 1970 with the introduction of the 1750 Kamm tail with its revised windscreen rake and shortened bodyshell. All subsequent Spiders derived from this model. Many of the changes carried out are detailed in other parts of this book.

Long tail Spiders
1600 Spider/Duetto 1966-1967

Number built: 6324

Model/chassis number: 105.03, RHD 105.05. Engine prefix: 536

Performance: Max power 109bhp (125bhp SAE) @ 6000rpm. Max speed 111mph (178kph). 0-60mph (97kph) 11.2 secs. Max torque 103lb/ft @ 2800rpm.

Engine: 1570cc, 4-cylinder water cooled in-line. All-aluminium alloy construction with cast iron liners. Hemispherical combustion chambers and twin overhead camshafts. Two double choke Weber 40-DCOE27 or Solex 40 C32PA1A7 carburettors. Bore & stroke 78 x 82mm. Compression ratio 9.1: 1.

Transmission: 5-speed all-syncromesh. Rear-wheel-drive. Gear ratios: 1st-3.30:1 2nd-1.99:1 3rd-1.35:1 4th-1.00:1 5th-0.790:1. Final drive 4.555:1.

Suspension: Front: independent with double wishbones, coil springs and telescopic dampers. Anti-roll bar. Rear: live axle with trailing arms, coil springs, T bracket, lower trailing arms, and telescopic shock absorbers.

Steering: recirculating ball or worm & roller.

Brakes: 4 wheel discs. Handbrake on rear wheels. Dunlop hydro-mechanical on early cars, no servo as standard. 1967. ATE branded with drum handbrake operating within rear calipers. Brake servo.

Electrics: 12v positive earth. Coil, distributor and dynamo. 14mm sparkplugs.

Dimensions: Overall length 167.3in (4250mm). Width 64.2in (1630mm). Height (with soft top erected) 51in (1295mm). Wheelbase 88.6in (2250mm). Front track 51.6in (1310mm). Rear track 50in (1270mm).

Wheels and tyres: 15 x 4½ J/155 SR 15. 4-stud steel bolt on wheels.

Kerb weight: 2182lb (990kg).

1750 Spider Veloce 1967-1969

Number built: See 1750 Kamm tail

Model/chassis number: 105.57 RHD 105.58 US:105.62. Engine prefix: 548 US: 551.

Performance: Max power 122bhp (132bhp SAE) @ 5500rpm; US: 115bhp (132bhp SAE) @ 5500rpm. Max speed 116mph (186kph). 0-60mph (97kph) 9.2secs; US 114mph (183kph) 9.9secs. Max torque 127lb/ft @ 2900rpm, US 137lb/ft @ 2800rpm (gross).

Engine: As per Duetto, but 1778cc, bore & stroke 80x 88.5mm. Compression ratio 9.5:1; US:9.0:1. Carburettors/injection Weber 40 DCOE32; US Alfa Spica Mechanical fuel-injection.

Transmission: As per Duetto but hydraulic clutch. Final drive 4.3: 1; US 4.55:1. ZF LSD optional.

Suspension: As per Duetto but rear anti-roll bar.

Brakes: As per late Duetto but larger discs, servo (US twin/dual circuit), pressure regulating valve.

Electrics: Alternator.

Dimensions: As per Duetto but US overall length 167.9in (4264mm). All: front track 52.1in(1323mm). Rear track 50.1in (1273mm).

Wheels and tyres: 14 x 5½ J/165 HR 14.

Kerb weight: 2292lb (1040kg). US 2346lb (1064kg).

All other data as per Duetto.

1300 Spider Junior 1968 -1969

Number built: 2680

Model/chassis number: 105.91 RHD 105.92 Engine Prefix: 530

Performance: Max power 89 bhp (103SAE) @6000rpm, Max speed 106mph (171kph), 0-60mph (97kph) 13 secs. Max torque:101lb ft @3200rpm.

Engine: As per Duetto, but: 1290 cc, carburettors Weber 40 DCOE28, Solex C40 DDH- 4or Dellorto DHLA

40. Bore & Stroke 74 x 75 mm. Compression ratio 9.0: 1.
Transmission: As per Duetto, but: 5th 0.860:1. Final drive 4.555:1 Clutch: hydraulic.
Suspension: As per 1750 SV brakes: As per late Duetto: servo standard 1969.
Electrics: As per Duetto. Dimensions: As per 1750 SV
Wheels and tyres: As per Duetto. Optional 14x5½J/165 SR14.
Kerb weight: 2182lb (990kg).
Electrics: As per Duetto.
All other data as per Duetto.

Kamm tail spiders
Series 2
1750 Spider Veloce 1970-1971
Number built: Kamm & long tail 4674, US: 4027.
Model/chassis number: 105.57 RHD 105.58 US: 105.62, Engine prefix: 548 US: 551.
Performance: Max power: 118bhp (132bhp SAE) @ 5500rpm, US: 135bhp gross @ 5500rpm
Max speed mph (kph): 116 (187) 0 – 60: 9.2secs (97kph), US:114 (183) 0-60: 9.9.
Max torque: 127lb/ft @ 2900rpm, US: 138lb/ft @ 2900rpm.
Engine: As 1750 LT but: compression ratio 9.1:1 US: 9.0:1
Transmission: As per 1750 LT. Final drive: 4.55:1
Brakes: As 1750 LT but dual circuit, 2x brake servo on all cars. Hanging pedals on LHD cars
Dimensions: As 1750 LT but: overall length 162.2in (4120mm) US: 169.9in (4315mm).
Wheels and tyres: As per 1750 LT
Kerb weight: 2260lb (1025kg) US: 2315lb (1050kg)
All other data as per 1750 LT.

1300 Spider Junior (1970-1977), 1600 Spider Junior/1600 Spider Veloce (1972-1981)
Number built: 1300: 4557, 1600: 4848.
Model/chassis number: 1300: 105.91, 1600: 115.07, 1974: 115.35.
Engine prefix: 1300: 530/ 1974 530*S. 1600: 536, 526A from 1974.
Performance: Max power: 1300: 89bhp (103bhp SAE) @ 6000rpm, 1600: 110bhp @ 6000rpm (125bhp SAE) 1974: 102bhp @ 5500rpm.
Max speed: 1300: 106mph (171kph) 0-60mph (97kph) 13 secs, 1600: 112mph (180kph) 11.3secs. Max torque:1300: 101lb/ft @ 3200rpm, 1600: 102lb/ft @ 2800rpm 1974 104lb/ft @ 2900rpm
Engine: As per previous 1300/1600 but: Compression ratio: 9. 01: 1, 1600 9.1:1.
Carburettors: 1300: Weber 40DCOE28, Dellorto DHLA40, Solex C40DDH-4.
1600: Weber 40 DCOE27, Dellorto DHLA40, Solex C40DDH-6.
Transmission: As per 1300 LT & Duetto but: final drive 1600 4.3:1 (1971-4).
Wheels and tyres: 15x4½J/ 155 SR15. Optional 14 x 5½J/165 SR 14.
Kerb weight: 1300: 2182lb (990kg) 1600: 2247lb (1019kg).
All other data as 1750 KT. 1600 SV identical to 2000SV.

2000 Spider Veloce 1971 –1982
Niki Lauda 1978 (US), Enthusiast's Spider 1982(US)
Number built: 16,320, US: 22,059
Model/chassis number: 105.24. 1975: 115.38 RHD: 105.27 (To 1977.) US: 115.02.1977 115.410.
Engine prefix: 512.1975 515. US: 01500 1982: 1544.
Performance: Max power: 132bhp @ 5500rpm (150bhp SAE) 1975 128bhp @ 5300rpm (147bhp SAE)

	Euro spec	1973 US	1977 US	1980 US	1982 US
* SAE net	see above	129 @5800*	111 @ 5000*	111 @5000*	115 @ 5500 *
Max speed mph (kph)	118 (190)	110 (177)	106 (170)	110 (177)	110 (177)
0-60sec (97kph)	8.9	11	10	10.7	11.7
Max torque lb/ft/rpm	132 @ 3500	132 @ 3500	122 @ 4000	116 @ 2500	119 @ 2750

Engine: As before but: 1962cc, bore & stroke 84 x 88.5m, compression ratio 9.5:1 US: 9.0:1 catalyst added 1977.1980 VVT (US only).
Carburettors/injection: Weber 40DCOE32, Dellorto DHLA40, Solex C40DDH.
US: Alfa Spica mechanical 1982 Bosch L Jetronic fuel injection.

Transmission: As before but: LSD as standard. Final drive 4.1:1 US: 4.55:1 1980 4.1:1.
Electrics: As before. 1980 electronic ignition. US: 1982 trunk mounted battery.
Dimensions: Length: 162.2in/4120mm, US: 1974 169.9in/4315mm, 1975-83 168.8in/4287mm
Wheels and tyres: 14 x 5½J/165 HR14/185/70 option from 1975. Alloys (option Euro).
US: Turbina alloys. 1982 6J x 14 Daytona alloys. 185/70 HR 14.
Kerb weight: 2292lb (1039kg) US: 2320lb (1052kg) 1977: 2430lb (1102kg) 1980: 2540lb (1152kg) 1982: 2495lb (1131kg).
All other data as per 1750KT.

Series 3/Aerodinamica

2000/1600 Spider/ Veloce 1983-1989, Quadrifoglio Verde (Green Cloverleaf) 1986-1989 Graduate (US) 1985
Number built: 10170 QV 2598, 1600: 5400, US: 19040 (All).
Model/chassis number: 2000 115.380(1983-1986), (1986) 115.660. QV 115.600. 1600: 115.35 (1983-1986) 115.62 (1986-1989) US 115.410, 115.75 QV 115.68.
Engine prefix: 2000 515, 1600: 526 & 526P, US: 01544.
Performance: Max power: 128bhp @ 5300rpm (147bhp SAE) 1600 104bhp @ 5500/5900rpm (1986) US: 115 @ 5500 SAE Net

	2000	**1600**	**US**
Max speed mph (kph)	118 (189)	112 (180)	110 (177)
0-60(97kph) sec	10	11.5	11.7
Max torque lbft/rpm	132 @ 4400	105 @ 2900/101 @ 4300(86)	119 @ 2750

Engine: As before 2000 & 1600, but 2000 Euro compression ratio 9.0:1.
Carburettors/injection: Weber 40DCOE32, Dellorto DHLA40, Solex C40DDH5.
1600: Weber 40 DCOE33 US: Bosch L Jetronic Fuel injection US: VVT & catalyst.
Transmission: As 2000 & 1600 Junior.
Electrics: As before 1984 electronic ignition 2000 Euro: 1984.1600/86.
Dimensions: Length: 168in (4267mm) US: 168.8in (4287mm).
Wheels and Tyres: 14 x 5½J/ 185/70 HR14. Alloys 2000SV (option Euro), 6J x 14 Daytona, QV Campagnolo 6J x 15/ 195/ 60R15.
Kerb weight: 2292lb (1040kg) 1600: 2247lb (1019kg) US: 2495lb (1133kg).
All other data as1750KT.

Series 4 Spiders

2000 Spider/Veloce 1990-1993 1600 Spider 1990-1992
Special Editions. Beute US: 1994 Commerative Edition
Number built: 18456 1600: 2951
Model/chassis number: 115/A1, 115/A1A catalyst, 1600: 115/A2.
Engine prefix: 01590, 01588 catalyst, 1600: 01563.
Performance:

	2000	**with catalyst**	**1600**
Max power: bhp/rpm	126 @ 5800	120 @ 5800	109 @ 6000
Max speed mph (kph):	119 (191)	118 (189)	112 (180)
0-60 mph (97 kph).sec	9.4	10.8	10.00
Max torque lb/ft/rpm	124 @ 4200	118 @ 4200	101 @ 4800
Engine: as per 2000/1600 but: compression ratio	10:1	10:1 (US 9.0:1)	9.0:1

Carburettors/injection: Bosch Motronic MI 4.1 I. 1600: Weber 40 DCO4/5. 2000 has VVT.
Transmission: As before but: final drive 4.1:1 1600: 4.55:1. US: only ZF 3 speed automatic ratios 1st 2.48, 2nd 1.48, 3rd 1.00.
Steering: ZF power assisted
Electrics: As before but electronic ignition 1600.
Dimensions: Length: All 167.6in (4257mm)
Wheels and tyres: 1600 14 X 5½J/ 185/70 HR14. 2000SV Campagnolo: 6J X 15/195/ 60 R15. US 2000 1990 steel wheels: 14 X 5½K 185/70 HR14.
Curb weight: 2445lb (1110kg), 2550lb catalyst (1156kg), 1600: 2357lb (1069kg).
All other data as per 1750 Kamm tail.

This data was compiled from various sources, including Alfa Romeo publications and archive, together with contemporary road tests by *Motor, Autocar, MotorSport, Car & Driver, Road & Track, Sports Car Graphic* and *Road Test*.

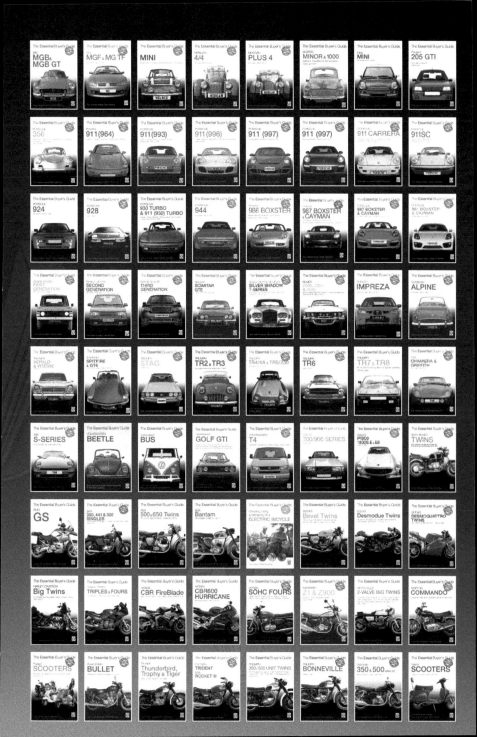

Index